STEALING FREEDOM

Vivien Patterson

D1730479

AMBASSADOR INTERNATIONAL
Greenville, South Carolina • Belfast, Northern Ireland

Stealing Freedom

© Copyright 2009 Vivien Patterson

ISBN 978-1-84030-211-0

Ambassador Publications
a division of
Ambassador Productions Ltd.
Providence House
Ardenlee Street,
Belfast,
BT6 8QJ
Northern Ireland
www.ambassador-productions.com

Emerald House
427 Wade Hampton Blvd.
Greenville
SC 29609, USA
www.emeraldhouse.com

In Memory Of
Mary

One day I shall see her again.

CONTENTS

FOREWORD

"Auntie Vivien ... will you take me to school please?" You will have to read the rest of the book to understand the impact of those special words spoken to the author; words that speak of the faithfulness of God, of restoration, freedom and healing. Vivien relates to us her journey in life that travels with tragedy and family traumas including suicide, mental disorder and separation from loved ones lasting 30 years. These have not been her only companions. For God entered her life in a personal way while she was in her late teens; a decade later she met her husband and in ensuing years four sons were born. Her joy filled marriage, friends and ministries have combined with those pains of the past to teach her, as she puts it, "what it means to live in the reality of God's presence each day and to be increasingly aware of the freedom that brings."

This book is an honest and open-hearted account of the author's experience that touches everyday life and living with its ups and downs, fears and even despairs. There are practical insights and personal stories, tinged with humour, that will ring true to the reader and provide real encouragement to journey on with faith placed in the One who is true freedom.

Issues surface that we may all face whether with God, oneself or others. Does God inflict such painful circumstances upon us? Where do our loyalties lie in family life?

That the Lord wants, through His grace and love, to answer our questions or speak into our situations is made so wonderfully clear whether using a husband, friend or Christian author but the priority of God's Word in its daily challenge and power to meet the need is given rightful prominence. Above all this book points us to the sufficiency of Christ for life, for living, for being or for doing no matter what the circumstances, to free us first for Him and then for others.

Mark Thomas
Managing Director
Capernwray Hall

INTRODUCTION

"The hardness of God is kinder than the softness of men and His compulsion is our liberation."

C S LEWIS

There is a creative energy born out of suffering and pain, which can transcend the human condition. When channelled positively, this energy becomes a powerful compelling force, which God in His infinite compassion longs to release through His children. It is essentially a creative energy birthed in God's sovereign love, springing from His heart and nurtured by His Holy Spirit. It has the potential to deliver us from our inability to journey on, unable to do so because our hearts have been crushed and our spirits overwhelmed by the cares of this world. Once the raw reality of pain has run its course and we embrace completely this God-given energy, we are able to enter into that realm of healing and wholeness which is totally liberating. There, we become fully alive and there, the enemy can no longer steal our freedom.

"So if the Son sets you free, you will be free indeed...."
(John 8:36)

A PERSONAL WORD

I would like to invite you, my reader, on a journey. It is a personal, intimate journey, during which I share my heart with you; my joys my pains. It is a journey which I have to share – indeed I long to share, for I cannot contain the reality of it any longer.

So I offer you my story. My prayer is that God will take these words which He has given me and use them to encourage your heart, so that you and I might travel a little further towards that place of complete security and freedom in Christ.

"It is for freedom that Christ has set us free. Stand firm then and do not let yourselves be burdened again by a yoke of slavery." (Gal. 5:1)

Acknowledgments

I am very grateful to Lynda Neilands, Pam Johnston, Kim Lee, Dave Jackson, Martha Bastke and Mark Thomas for their expert advice and encouragement which they have willingly given to me whilst I have been undertaking this venture.

My special thanks also to my family and friends in Bristol, Northern Ireland and the Isle of Man, but particularly to my husband, Trevor. His integrity, constant love, loyal support and humour have helped to keep me grounded for many years.

1

RECOLLECTIONS

"There's nothing wrong my dear…… go back to sleep." My mother's voice penetrated the stillness of the night, for I had been wrestling with sleep for several hours. The following morning, I studied her haunted, tormented face as she told me that she had come into my room during the night to kill me.

"I had steeled myself to do it," she explained. "I was going to use the chopper from the garage, but I was worried that the police were watching me, so I came into your room to check that you were asleep, but you woke up. So I waited…. but I must have fallen asleep myself. I had to kill you my dear……you will not be able to cope with the persecution you see…..I must protect you from that fate."

Several hours later and after consultation with the police, social workers, the GP and the consultant psychiatrist, I found myself signing papers in order for my desperately sick, widowed mother to be admitted under section, to the local psychiatric hospital in Bristol. During that day, I had overheard words such as paranoia and psychosis being used by the professionals. A diagnosis to this effect was later confirmed. However, that was in 1967 and I was just 22 years old…..

One of the drawbacks of living with a person with a severe mental disorder is that the symptoms are potentially contagious, because the paranoia which torments the patient also affects close family members. Being constantly reminded that "people were watching me" does eventually have a conditioning effect, causing uneasiness and chipping away at self-esteem. Certainly my ability to form normal healthy relationships was impaired.

After the incident described, leading to my mother being hospitalized for six months, she came home and with the help of medication, trod a very delicate line between some kind of normality and increasingly strange behaviour. At the same time, she was aiming to hold down a very demanding secretarial post, her intelligence never having been in question. Aware of my responsibility to care for her and also conscious of a very real and deep love for her, I struggled at juggling my career as a teacher with supporting her as much as I could. Whenever her illness caused her thinking to become distorted again, I would try to speak truth into her life.

However, the abnormal was slowly becoming the normal for me and this hit home the hardest whenever I left Bristol in the summer holidays to work in youth camps. It increasingly became difficult to readjust from the one environment to the other. It took years before I discovered that it is almost impossible to redress the balance and reason with a person whose mind has succumbed to the devastating effects of mental illness. So it was only a matter of time, when on the advice of her consultant psychiatrist, I moved from the family home to a small flat close by, which offered me a measure of independence and protection and yet I was on hand should she need me.

Looking for me, it was to that same flat one Saturday morning in December 1969 that my mother ran, in her bedroom slippers and without her coat. She banged on my door, uncertain of catching me since I had planned to go to Birmingham for the weekend.

"She's done it, she's done it!" she screamed. "Mary's dead! She's killed herself!"

Mary was my only sister and we had no brothers. She had trained as a nurse in Bristol and married Jonathan, an accountant and fellow Bristolian on a rather chilly November day in 1965. I was a student in Birmingham at the time and travelled home to Bristol that particular weekend for the wedding, looking forward very much to being her bridesmaid. Mary and Jonathan began married life in the North of England. They were very happy and after two years Mary gave birth to their first child, a son named Paul. In terms of my mother's illness, I could not have managed without my sister. She was extremely supportive and being a nurse, she probably had more insight into my mother's condition than I had.

About a year after Paul's birth, Mary and Jonathan moved to a little village near Gloucester, partly so that they were nearer Bristol and could offer more support during any impending crisis with my mother. I appreciated their help so much. Mary was very wise and balanced in her thinking and we spent many hours discussing the situation and the best way to cope with it. Jonathan continued his career as a chartered accountant, working for a local firm in the Gloucester area.

After the birth of their second son Ian, Mary changed. We now know that she suffered from severe postnatal depression. However, in the sixties the illness did not have anything like the same focus or high profile that it has today. There was far less recognition or understanding of the symptoms and little professional expertise available. As a family we were certainly aware that Mary was ill because her behaviour had become increasingly irrational. We didn't really know how to cope and we just hoped and prayed that it would pass. She was weighed down by oppression and she had become severely introverted. We had heard of the "baby blues," but this was extreme. About a month before she died, she had overdosed and had been admitted to hospital. However, the following day, she discharged herself. As a precaution, Jonathan removed all medication from the bathroom cabinet and the keys from doors. She was due to see a psychiatrist, but two days before the appointment, she sent Jonathan to the village shop to buy washing powder and encouraged him to take Paul along, as the two year old would enjoy the outing with his father. When they returned, Jonathan heard Ian crying in his cot and sensing something was wrong, found Mary in the bedroom. She had chosen a violent death.

Her funeral was inevitably a blur to me and I remember very little. In the weeks that followed, Jonathan and I drew very close. We wept together; we clung to each other and I witnessed his anguish as in silence we cleared up the bedroom where Mary had died.

After her death, Jonathan and his two little sons went to live with his sister Gill, who was married with a young family of her own. She was a wonderful substitute mother for Paul and Ian; extremely warm and loving and her Italian husband Thomas was very supportive. The wider family circle also gave a great deal of help and I was one of many close relatives who frequently spent time with Paul and Ian, taking them on outings and generally caring for them. My mother, when she was well enough, took Paul to nursery school and they formed a special bond as hand in hand, they walked the short distance to the school each day.

As time passed, I was aware that Jonathan was becoming increasingly friendly with Sharon, an old school friend of Mary's. However, nothing had prepared me for the decision which they eventually made. In 1971, almost two years to the day after Mary had died, Jonathan and Sharon announced that they were leaving England and beginning a new life abroad. They would be taking Paul and Ian with them as well as Jennie, Sharon's daughter from a previous marriage. They would not be returning. They would not be giving us their new address and we were not to try to find them. Then they left. Sharon cut the ties with her family and Jonathan with his. Gill, who had cared so tenderly for little Paul and Ian, was totally devastated as was the whole family. No one knew where they had gone. Eventually, we discovered that Jonathan and Sharon had married. They were living somewhere in Africa with the children and Jonathan was working as an accountant. We knew no more than that and certainly were unaware when we would see the children again, if ever.

My mother could not cope with losing her grandchildren as well as her daughter. She suffered another major breakdown and was admitted to hospital yet again.

2

Rugby, Tears ... and a Revelation

"You will seek me and find me when you seek me with all your heart." (Jeremiah 29.13)

As a seventeen year old, growing up at the time when every teenage girl dreamed of marrying Elvis Presley, I certainly never imagined that I would be singing hymns on a Saturday night, at a place called Lee Abbey. But that's where I found myself! It was Easter 1963 and I had been invited by my close school friend, Hazel, to a sixth form conference at the Centre. Hazel was a Christian, although I had little understanding as to what that really meant. All I knew was that she had a strong faith and possessed a certain wisdom and composure. There was a presence about her and a peace in her life, yet she was great fun and I knew that I could trust her.

My parents were God fearing, good living people. They were very happily married and they gave my sister and me a loving and secure home. I had been brought up as an Anglican, christened as a baby and confirmed at the age of fourteen, a year after my sister Mary. After that, my teenage years brought with them the normal insecurities and hormonal changes characteristic of that period of youth, plus a healthy questioning of the deeper significance of life. I think I swung from seeing myself as a tambourine-playing captain in the Salvation Army, working in their soup kitchens, to being a fully paid up card-carrying member of the local Atheistic Society, my allegiance being totally coloured by the mood of the moment. Where ever my loyalty lay, I certainly believed in having a good time, whether that was partying or spending Tuesday nights at Bristol Jazz Club. We danced to the live music of Acker Bilk, Kenny Ball and his Jazzmen and George Melly. It was the highlight of the week, the Mecca for all young Bristolians and we loved it. It was there that as teenagers, we would take our first tentative steps towards the uncertain, but curiously enticing world of the opposite sex.

And then my father died…It happened about six months before my visit to Lee Abbey and without my realizing that it was imminent. Certainly, I was aware that his on-going heart condition had weakened him, but I was not prepared for the massive heart attack which so suddenly and cruelly took him from us, when he was only in his mid-fifties. My father, whom I adored, on whom I leaned more than perhaps I realised and who I thought would live for ever, was gone. This man of wisdom and compassion, whose integrity before God had given me such a solid and secure start in life was no longer with us. My mind drifts back to the times when as a family, we would take a picnic and drive in our Austin Seven to a favourite spot in the country, often the Wye Valley. I recall on more than one occasion, my father would gaze at the beautiful scenery and be moved to tears.

"Isn't this wonderful Viv!" I can almost hear his voice now and see him wiping his cheek with his handkerchief. Aware that my father longed to share his enthusiasm with me, I remember that I would slip my hand into his and try as a young child, to work up a similar sense of wonder. I desperately wanted to enter his world, feel the emotion he felt and value as passionately as he did the magnificence of creation. However, my youthful desire to stand alongside him and unite with him, inevitably gave way to a totally inadequate and under-developed awareness of the beauty of nature... and I would fail miserably. Smith's crisps and my favourite sandwiches would win my approval, gain my attention every time and take priority over any reaction to meandering rivers and rolling hills.

Appreciating the countryside so deeply was not the only experience to move my father to tears. He was a rugby man and although born and bred in Bristol, had fostered strong Welsh connections especially during his school years. He was very pleased when I introduced him to my first boyfriend, Colin, whom I had met at the Jazz Club and who played rugby for the under eighteens Bristol squad. My father took great delight in explaining the rules of the game to me so that I could support Colin at his matches and our relationship might become more meaningful. (Not that I ever fully grasped the finer points of the game....What exactly is a ruck?) However, the friendship came to an end when Colin went to University. The Five Nations Rugby Tournament was the highlight of the rugby season in our home. Now of course, it has become the Six Nations Rugby Tournament, with the inclusion more recently of Italy. Each year, my father would watch it avidly on our twelve inch black and white television set. We hardly dared breath, let alone speak during those matches, as he would enter totally into the game, becoming increasingly animated and vocal with the state of play and switching his assumed role of scrum-half to referee, whenever he felt that his assistance was needed. The climax of the tournament for him was always the Wales-England match. Before the kick-off, as thousands of passionate Welshmen raised their voices in harmony to sing "Land of my Fathers," I would study my father, as his eyes filled with tears…. All these years later, I cannot watch the Wales-England match without a huge sense of nostalgia and affection for the father who was irreplaceable. …And yes, when the Welsh begin to sing, I still find it difficult to hold back the tears.

In his book, "Surprised by Joy," C.S.Lewis writes poignantly about the death of his mother, which he tragically experienced as a young child. The account is both beautiful and graphic. He describes seeing his mother's body as being extremely traumatic for him and I expected that my reaction to death would be similar. I remember going to the Chapel of Rest with my mother and sister, two days after my father had died. I had never seen anyone in a coffin before and I steeled myself to go through the ordeal. However, all I can say is that for me it was a revelation. My response totally took me by surprise, as I became aware that I was looking at a shell…. The man who was my father, so alive, so strong and dependable, so warm and tenderhearted, just wasn't there. As I look back to that day, I believe my spiritual life was awakened at that very moment. Birthed in me, was an awareness of the need to see this present life in the light of eternity. The stark contrast between life and death was very real and I knew that I would never be the same again.

During the next few months leading up to my visit to Lee Abbey, I struggled with adapting to life without my father. Mary and I drew closer, gaining strength from each other and together we witnessed my mother's grief, as she bravely fought to regain control of her life. She was in her mid-forties when she was widowed and outwardly, she courageously maintained a quiet dignity, which won the respect of many. She insisted that we make no change to our future plans. I was not, as I suggested, to think of transferring my college place from Birmingham to Bristol and Mary was to continue her studies as a nurse.

To some extent, I think I internalised my grief and in time, carried on with my life almost as if nothing had happened .The Jazz Club and partying became high on my list of priorities again, as I sought to fill the void in the only way I knew how at that stage. However, my thinking continued to be disturbed by the revelation which took place at the Chapel of Rest. I believe now that God in His grace and compassion, was nurturing the seed which He had sown in my mind .He was tenderly allowing it to take root, as I became more and more unsettled with what the world offered me in terms of superficial fulfilment and yet increasingly aware of issues concerning eternity.

It was in this frame of mind that I arrived at Lee Abbey, a Christian community centre run by the Anglican Church and situated near Lynton, North Devon. The scenery is quite breathtaking. The Abbey is perched on the cliffs overlooking Lee Bay and it can only be approached by driving through the Valley of Rocks. The centre runs many house parties, but the sixth form conference was an annual event, taking place over the Easter period and still does, as far as I know. It was not the teaching which challenged me, but the quality and character of the young people who were staying there. I became conscious of a reality to their lives which was quite new to me. Many spoke of a living, vibrant, intimate relationship with Jesus, of which I knew nothing and they did so in a way that was quite natural. Certainly they appeared to be well-balanced, normal young people, not weird or freakish in any way. I was so impressed with their warmth and their love of life and I was greatly challenged by this new dimension of freedom and security, which their relationship with Jesus seemed to bring them. Leaving the conference the following Saturday, I remember one young man making this statement,

"Of course, we tend to think that God is only real at Lee Abbey, but that's not true. We don't leave Him behind. He's with us all the time." Those words stayed with me; also Hazel's response when I shared with her that I was aware of a wonderful atmosphere during the week. "That was the presence of the Holy Spirit," she said. New thinking for me! In the weeks which followed, I found myself increasingly drawn to the Bible and to Christian literature and I was aware of a particular need to make sense of what was meant by the Trinity. The person and character of Jesus especially intrigued me. I began to realise that my understanding of His identity was not only incredibly limited, but also distorted. Somewhere in my thinking, I had come to accept that the Gospels were true historically, but in terms of the crucifixion, I had perceived Jesus to be a victim. Certainly at that stage, I had no real concept of Him being God incarnate and in any case, how could a victim help me to gain a handle on my life? Then, in my searching, I discovered this powerful Scripture. Luke 9:51 states,

"As the time approached for Him to be taken up to heaven, Jesus resolutely set out for Jerusalem." His decision! John10:17-18, also helped to shed light on the matter. Here, Jesus makes this very clear statement. *"The reason my Father loves me is that I lay down my life….only to take it up again .No one takes it from me, but I lay it down of my own accord. I have authority to lay it down and I have authority to take it up again. This command I received from my Father."* These verses linked His death, with His resurrection and spoke of Jesus being in control over both. The pursuit of truth was now driving me. Some weeks later, it culminated in my responding to an

overwhelming awareness of the love of God for me, as expressed first and foremost by His Son on the cross. I saw for the first time, why Jesus came to this broken bleeding world. Out of obedience to His Father, He chose to die for mankind, so that through His sacrificial death and resurrection, we might know forgiveness and be reconciled to God. There was much of course, that I did not yet understand. But for the first time in my life, I felt God's closeness. It was almost as if my world was no longer two- dimensional, but three-dimensional. My roots were in firmer soil and I felt more secure, more grounded. In sensing God's closeness, I became conscious of a new identity which was somehow wrapped up in my growing awareness of God's presence in my life and of His love for me. I was experiencing a freedom to be myself and also potentially, to be the person God had created me to be. It seems to me that once we know the reality of God in our lives, nothing else can compete or satisfy. When God breathes life into dry bones, His Spirit not only touches, but embraces the human spirit at its deepest level. Out of that certainty, an energy arises which affects the core of man's identity and colours his every experience. He is truly reborn.

In his book "Mere Christianity," C.S.Lewis makes this statement,

"It is when I turn to Christ, when I give myself up to His personality, that I first begin to have a real personality of my own." I guess that's what I was starting to experience at the tender age of seventeen and it thrilled me. My world became full of colours, which I had never really noticed before, or allowed to affect my thinking, but which expressed so perfectly, in a verse from this beautiful old hymn…

"Heaven above is softer blue,
Earth around is sweeter green.

Something lives in every hue,
Christless eyes have never seen:
Birds with gladder songs o'erflow,
Flowers with deeper beauties shine
Since I know, as now I know,
I am His, and He is mine."

Much to my joy, Mary also responded to the message of the Gospel, as the result of a series of evangelistic meetings taking place in Bristol. We both began to go to church again on a regular basis (for Mary, it was as her nursing duties allowed) but how wonderful to enjoy this newfound fellowship with my sister! That September, I left Bristol for Birmingham to train to be a teacher, returning to Bristol in the summer of 1966, when I began my teaching career at a local primary school.

I have already touched on events surrounding the next few years. In between the trauma of losing my sister, Jonathan disappearing with Paul and Ian and my mother's recurring illness, I tried, with varying degrees of success, to live a comparatively normal life. I love the theatre and in my early twenties, joined the Bristol Old Vic Theatre Club. I became a regular theatre-goer, enjoying plays which were of an exceptionally high standard and after a trial season in Bristol, were frequently transferred to London's West End. I miss being able to do that now, which is why it is such a treat to go to London for the occasional weekend, armed with tickets for a West End show, or maybe even two shows! At its best, there is something quite amazing about live theatre; the hush of anticipation and excitement in the auditorium as the lights dim and the curtain is raised. For one marvellous evening, you are transported to another world and everything else pales into insignificance, compared with the drama which is unfolding before your eyes and the characters on-stage, who temporarily have become part of your life. Brilliant!

During those years in Bristol and in keeping with my love of the theatre, amateur dramatics became a favourite pastime and I also dabbled in oil painting when the mood was right. The latter, along with dance drama, had been my two main subjects at college. In terms of my career, I was enjoying teaching; it was extremely demanding, but it certainly gave some stability and routine to the day. My headmaster was very supportive, as were my colleagues. Some became exceptionally close friends, especially Ann and Brian, whose two little boys were roughly the same age as Paul and Ian. Before Jonathan took his sons away, the four youngsters would play happily together on some of the occasions when I was looking after my nephews. Ann and Brian welcomed me into their home as if I was family. We are still close today and I thank God for them and for their kindness to me.

On Sundays, I started to attend a small open Brethren Assembly in Lawrence Weston, Bristol and also help with the youth work during the week. But from time to time, my roots drew me back to a local Anglican church, where the teaching was extremely good and from where some years later, I was eventually married.

Life continued along these lines until 1973, when events at home were proving difficult again and taking their toll on my fragile ability to cope. In the summer of that year, at the end of a challenging school term, I drove northwards in my red Mini, towards Sheffield and a place which meant a great deal to me... Cliff College.

3

A Lesson in Relinquishment

*"I sought the Lord and He answered me; He delivered me
from all my fears."(Psalm 34.4)*

Cliff College was established over one hundred years ago and at
the time when I was visiting, primarily provided training for
students wishing to enter the Methodist Ministry. My
experience there was quite literally life changing. The
connection with the College was through a teaching colleague,
whose father was the Administrator and I had stayed there on
two or three occasions, as a guest of the family. In July 1973, I
arrived at the College for the Derwent Convention, held every
year and open to the general public. Outwardly, I gave the
impression of being in complete control of my life and of my
circumstances, but inwardly the reality was very different. All
awareness of God's presence had left me and I was struggling
with a deep sense of fear and anguish.I felt consumed by
darkness and engulfed by the devastating effects which

depression had had on my family, causing Mary's death and my mother's irrational behaviour. I was terrified that I would be the next one to succumb to its evil clutches; it was only a matter of time. The thought of returning home to Bristol paralysed me. I envisaged myself driving passed the house and round the block several times, before finding the courage to turn my key in the lock and go in, not knowing in what state of mind I would find my mother. Unable to face the prospect of returning to a situation, where her behaviour was frequently unpredictable and where I was constantly being fed lies about people plotting against us, I began to spiral downwards, towards a level of total despair.

The speaker at Cliff College that week was a Baptist pastor from Scotland. His teaching sessions each day were from Luke.4:18-19.

"The Spirit of the Lord is on me because He has anointed me to preach good news to the poor. He has sent me to proclaim freedom for the prisoners and recovery of sight for the blind, to release the oppressed, to proclaim the year of the Lord's favour."

As he spoke from these verses, I sensed a stirring in my spirit and a new hope being born in my heart that perhaps these words were for me. Certainly the darkness I had known began to give way to a little light, as the truth of God's Word was brought to us with such insight, authority and compassion. I am reminded of when the Psalmist wrote,

"The unfolding of your words gives light; it gives understanding to the simple." (Psalm 119; 130) and that's exactly what happened. Never before had I understood so clearly this prophetic Word from Luke's Gospel. Never before had I received the truth of these verses into my spirit. Never before had I allowed Scripture to take root and become part of the life within, to such an extent. Never before had I been so

conscious that here was a minister, who perhaps by God's grace, could help me deal with my inner turmoil. And so with some apprehension, but no doubt in my mind that it was the right, I sought out the pastor.

He listened patiently to my story and then with words which I believe came straight from the heart of God, he began to minister to me. He did not believe that God had inflicted my circumstances upon me, but that my situation came within the realm of God's permissive will; God had allowed certain events to take place. The pastor seemed to understand my dilemma and he touched the reality of my pain and confusion in a way that helped me to feel totally safe with him. He explained that it was important to give up fighting God and to trust Him even in the middle of the heartache. Somehow, however difficult it might be, I had to learn to say "Yes" to the Father heart of God, resting in His sovereign love and assurance of protection and deliverance.

As I struggled with all that this godly man was saying, I found myself reacting negatively.

"I can't do that." I said. "I'm not able to do that. It's too difficult."

"I understand," he replied. He then suggested that he would pray and I was to repeat the words after him. That seemed acceptable. The prayer was very simple. The words were authoritative, yet full of compassion and I was able to repeat them. As the pastor and I bowed our heads and were in agreement before God in acknowledging His permissive will in my life, something very powerful happened. I found myself able to relinquish the heaviness of heart and soul which had weighed me down for so long. It just lifted and in doing so, I experienced such a release in my spirit and an overwhelming sense of the presence of God, as He filled me with His love and His peace. I cannot explain the mystery of how this happened, except to say that it did happen and I am thankful for it. As I write these words, verses from Isaiah 61 spring to mind. Luke. 4:18-19 is of course a reference to Jesus reading from this passage in Isaiah. As we know, Jesus was fulfilling Old Testament prophesy and I have heard it suggested that Isaiah 61:1-3 is God's mission statement to mankind, accomplished through His Son.

"The spirit of the Sovereign Lord is upon me, because the Lord has anointed me to preach good news to the poor. He has sent me to bind up the broken hearted, to proclaim freedom for the captives and release from darkness for the prisoners, to proclaim the year of the Lord's favour and the day of vengeance of our God, to comfort all who mourn and provide for those who grieve in Zion...to bestow on them a crown of beauty instead of ashes, the oil of gladness instead of mourning, and a garment of praise instead of a spirit of despair. They will be called oaks of righteousness, a planting of the Lord for the display of His splendour." (Isaiah 61:1-3)

In embracing the reality of this statement, I began to understand what was meant by these verses. The day that the Scottish pastor ministered to me, was the day God began to give me, just when I needed it,

"....a crown of beauty instead of ashes, the oil of gladness instead of mourning and a garment of praise instead of a spirit of despair." In one sense, nothing had changed. My circumstances were exactly the same. But I had changed. I returned to Bristol aware that God had touched my life and I could rest in the freedom of knowing that I could trust Him again.

In my new found peace I was able to look forward to a holiday in Israel three weeks later, a holiday that would introduce me to my future husband...Such is the providential timing of Almighty God.

4

An Unexpected Encounter

*"For I know the plans I have for you, declares the Lord, plans
to prosper you and not to harm you, plans to give you hope
and a future." (Jeremiah 29.11)*

It was August, 1973 and our last night in the Holy Land. The
young man sitting next to me was certainly not tall, dark and
handsome. He was short, quite stocky and with a hair line which
was beginning to recede. I had noticed him more than once
during our two week stay in Jerusalem, but we had spent little
time in each other's company. A large group making up the
house party was from Northern Ireland. Trevor was one of them.
I was attracted by his easy manner, his warmth and his humour.
But on a deeper level, I sensed that he was a man of strong
character and integrity. As I gathered my thoughts towards him
that night, I remember being surprised by my reaction because I
found myself praying quite naturally,

"Father, he's your child. He belongs to you. Do not let me be drawn to this young man, unless your hand is on our relationship. I release him to you."

I had never prayed that prayer before, although over the past few years, boyfriends had come and gone and one or two had been longstanding friendships. Later, that same evening, Trevor gave me a Bible bound in leather and olive wood. It was a totally unexpected gift and he offered me no real explanation as to the gesture.

On the return flight to England the next day, my girlfriends who by now were in full match-making mode, encouraged me to sit in the empty passenger seat next to him.

"He gave you a Bible for goodness sake Viv! Sit next to him; it would be rude not to do so." Jan prodded me in the right direction and feeling a little presumptuous, I responded. I had tried to argue with her, that there was little point beginning a friendship which could go nowhere, because Trevor and I lived so far apart, but she would have none of that. So he and I sat together for the seven hour journey back to England and although nothing specific was said, by the time we touched down at Luton Airport, we were both aware that our parting would be only temporary.

By Christmas of that same year we were engaged and the following summer, we were married. Between the time of our first meeting and our wedding day, I think we were reunited on no more than five occasions. The telephone bill was certainly excessive and the postman deserved a bonus, but in retrospect, I am very aware that we actually carried out most of our courtship after we were married. We were both more than conscious that God had called us to become husband and wife. In fact, it was one of those rare times when I felt that every fibre of my being was in tune with the will of God. However, Trevor and I faced a huge learning curve in terms of knowing how to express that God-given love. It is most definitely not a situation I would recommend outside of God's providence. English culture is very different from Irish culture; even more so in those days and initially I felt almost as if I had married the whole family.

I remember the first occasion I visited Northern Ireland, after having met Trevor. On the evening I arrived, his mother invited us for supper and I assumed I would simply be meeting his parents. Not so! The lounge was packed with family and extended family; relatives whose accents I could not understand and who were there, most definitely to give me the "once over." At least, that's how it felt at the time. There was a great deal of humour that evening. I'm not sure what everyone was laughing at, but I joined in whenever it seemed appropriate and I was certainly conscious of a close knit, warm and loving family. Trevor's younger brother, Alvin was particularly gregarious and very funny. I liked him immediately. Alvin's wife, Sandra, was extremely attractive and I felt that she was very sophisticated, although she would not agree with me. I liked her too. My future parents-in-law were kind and welcoming, as were the rest of the family. In true Irish fashion, an enormous supper had been prepared and I left their home that evening, feeling not only distinctly overwhelmed, but also distinctly overfed.

In the early days of our marriage, there were many reasons why I found adapting to life in Northern Ireland difficult. Some reasons were more obvious than others. Of course it involved a whole new identity for me, a new country, a new family (much larger than my own) a new teaching position and a new status as a wife. At 29 years of age, my independence had become increasingly important to me and now, I suddenly had to learn to make decisions with another person in mind; so had Trevor. However, these were not huge issues because we were both very sure of God's call on our lives and of the way He had brought us together.

By far the most difficult problem for me was leaving a widowed mother behind in Bristol, whom I felt still needed to lean on me. I constantly struggled with this dilemma. Trevor was surrounded by a warm, loving family, who embraced me whole-heartedly, but somehow that only made the comparison more difficult for me. I argued with God over His choice of husband.

"Why Trevor Lord? I know you have given me a deep love for him, but wouldn't it have been better for me to be married to someone from Bristol? Then I could still live locally and be around for my mother too." This conflict raged within me for a very long time. So much so that on occasions, I resented spending time with Trevor's family, even feeling swamped by them. His parents had never lost any close member of their family. How could they possibly understand how I felt? It all seemed so one-sided and unfair. The loser seemed to be my mother on every count. She had already lost a husband and a daughter. Two grandchildren had disappeared and her one remaining daughter, now living across the Irish Sea, was only able to spend time with her when she came to stay, or vice versa. A permanent move from Bristol to Ireland had always been treated with great caution by her doctor, whenever the subject was raised. I can see that my heart ruled my head in those days, but there were times when everything within me, heart, soul and mind, would cry out to God, "She needs me!"

It was like an open wound which refused to heal. Of course the inevitable happened and guilt set in. Call it misplaced guilt, false guilt, or the real thing, it is equally destructive, or it can be if it is not dealt with in the right way. Trevor struggled too. He knew how the situation affected me and he wanted to protect me. It was not always appropriate to go to Bristol whenever there was a crisis, but the anxiety I felt and the heaviness which would come over me at such times, caused him some resentment towards his mother-in-law. We rarely argued, but there would be a definite tension between us, despite the fact that we knew our marriage was solid.

Did my concerns negate the wise words of the pastor who ministered to me a few weeks before I met Trevor? I was more than conscious at that stage, of how God had touched my life and freed me from the dark place in which I found myself. Prior to that time, I was in no fit state of mind to carry out a courtship which would eventually lead to marriage. How could I learn to love, when I was consumed by fear? It would have been unreasonable to expect any man to deal with my pain; in fact it would have been impossible. I would have been wanting Trevor to give me what only God can give, which is true freedom, healing and wholeness. Thankfully, God began that process before we met. And of course it is very much a process. Human frailty is such that we tend to take two steps forward and one step back. In my limited thinking, moving from Bristol to Ireland only intensified my concerns and it would be a very long time before I began to understand what God was doing and to see the broader canvas.

During my thirties, my main vocation in life seemed to be having babies and by the time I was 39, Trevor and I were the proud parents of four sons. I was not aware of strong maternal feelings before I became a mother. I did not peer into prams or fuss over friends' babies, so the sense of fulfilment I experienced as our family grew in size, was something of a surprise for me. I loved being a housewife and mother. Having taught for eleven years, before our first son, Robert was born, I was ready to give up my job and be a full time mother. Certainly with four children under the age of six, I was aware that I could not be a good teacher and a good mum, so I never returned to teaching. Although I enjoyed my career (especially in Ireland) I have no regrets about that.

Every summer, Trevor and I plus four excited young boys, would pile into the family estate car, board the "Sea Cat" at Larne, land at Stranraer and drive down through Scotland, to Lancashire and Capernwray Hall. Here, we enjoyed countless wonderful holidays geared to families. There were plenty of activities for children and an opportunity for a complete rest for weary parents. Facilities are excellent and now include an indoor, heated swimming pool, sports hall, climbing wall, weights room, table tennis, tennis courts and of course, a football field.

Capernwray Hall is a large country house, standing in beautiful grounds in the heart of the Lancashire countryside. It is close to both the Lake District and the Yorkshire Dales. The Hall was purchased in 1946 by Major and Mrs. Ian Thomas, who believed that God's purpose for the property was to make it a place where young people could come and stay and be introduced to Christ. The first ten guests arrived in 1947 and since then, thousands have passed through its doors. During the academic year, it is a short term Bible College, but throughout the Christmas, Easter, and summer seasons, Capernwray offers weekly holiday programmes, catering for a mixed age range of young people, a cross section of adults and also families. Guests come from around the U.K. and across the world, giving it a truly international flavour.

There are now over twenty similar centres world-wide, coming under the umbrella of the Capernwray Missionary Fellowship of Torchbearers. During the family weeks, children are looked after extremely well, as are the parents, both having their own varied programmes of events. There is plenty of opportunity to be as private as you want to be, to explore the countryside all day, or to mix with other guests on campus and enjoy the amenities. The day begins and ends with relevant Bible teaching, provided by excellent guest speakers, who are encouraging and challenging. The children absolutely love the holiday, making friends from far and wide and being reunited with them each year. It is an extremely safe environment for them, which counts for so much in today's society. Perhaps you have heard of Capernwray, or have enjoyed staying there yourself. If you have, you will no doubt agree with me that it is a very special place. Certainly, our boys couldn't wait to return each year. Trevor and I loved it too and are still in touch with many of the friends we made there over the years. It has played a hugely significant part in our lives, not just because of good holidays, but more recently because it quite literally changed the direction in which we were moving. However, more of that later….

The Oscar winning film "Chariots of Fire" was on general release about the time that my boys were primary school age. As you probably know, the film tells the story of two fine athletes who competed in the Olympic Games, back in the nineteen twenties. They were Eric Liddell, a Christian and Harold Abrahams, a Jew.

Much has been made of the fact that Eric Liddell refused to compete in the heats, scheduled to take place on a Sunday. However, he went on to win a gold medal in an alternative race for which he had not initially trained, but which avoided Sunday heats. A statement which is credited to him and which says much about his relationship with God is as follows,

"God made me run and He made me fast. When I run, I feel God's pleasure." I am aware that it is a statement which has been well used to illustrate a point, but all I can say is that the first time I heard it, I was greatly challenged. I was attending a day conference for women, at a church in Belfast and the subject was "Fulfilment." The church was packed with women from all sorts of backgrounds and ages, but the vast majority of us were housewives and mothers. The speaker referred to this statement by Eric Liddell. She explained that although not one woman present was an Olympic athlete, we had all been gifted by God in many ways. As we offered our gifts to God, we too could feel His pleasure. She focused on the Scripture from Colossians 3.23,24.

"Whatever you do, work at it with all your heart, as working for the Lord and not for men, since you know that you will receive an inheritance from the Lord as a reward. It is the Lord Christ you are serving."

At that stage in my life, much of my day was taken up with mundane tasks, encompassing endless housework, along with meeting the demands of four young children. Some of the time I think I just muddled through, almost drowning in a sea of nappies, odd socks and Lego. In seeking to take on board the truth of this Scripture, I began to see that however basic and boring the task, it was immediately lifted to a higher plain if I could learn to offer it to God, as an act of service. Whenever I remembered to do this, it really helped me to see that washing dishes, peeling potatoes, tidying the home, was of value to God and that I too, could feel His pleasure. For was God not my Father, who loved me and cared for my boys as only He could? I believe that Isaiah 40:11 is a verse for mothers and their children.

"He tends His flock like a shepherd. He gathers the lambs in is arms and carries them close to His heart; He gently leads those that have young."

There is no better place than dwelling close to the heart of God. It is without doubt, the safest, most secure place to be.

5

STANLEY AND HAGGAI

"The Lord your God, who is going before you, will fight for you, as He did for you in Egypt, before your very eyes, and in the desert .There you saw how the lord your God carried you, as a father carries his son, all the way you went until you reached this place."(Deut.1. 30-31)

During the 1980's, Trevor and I were involved in a home group in our area. The members of the group came from all sorts of backgrounds, but over the months and years we had drawn very close. One particular Monday night, Trevor had invited us to share prayer requests. Events in Bristol were again proving difficult and I was heavy hearted. I shared very simply that I would value prayer for my family situation in Bristol and after a moment of quietness Stanley spoke up. Dear Stanley, Trevor's closest friend, our worship leader and a very godly man. He told me that he believed God had given him a verse for me. At that stage in my Christian experience I was not really used to this phenomenon and may have been more dismissive if I hadn't had such respect for the man. Stanley referred to Haggai 2: 5

"This is what I covenanted with you when you came out of Egypt. And my Spirit remains among you. Do not fear."

Stanley explained that he had no idea what the verse would mean to me, but believed in his spirit that it was a word from God for me.

The one word which caught hold of me was 'Egypt.' I understand that in Scripture, Egypt can be interpreted in more than one way. It can refer to the whole area of disobedience, but I am also aware that it can equally represent bondage. What was God saying to me?

Could Egypt in some way refer symbolically to Bristol? If that was the case, then the verse was extremely reassuring. The weight of turmoil and inner pain could hopefully be laid down in the knowledge that God ultimately had His Hand on the whole situation and was working out His purposes. Did Egypt refer to the hold which Bristol still had on my life in terms of how I saw my duty to my mother, my love for her and how that was worked out in practical terms? My dilemma was how to maintain the balance between Bristol and Ireland and fulfil my responsibilities to both. It was of course right to embrace family ties in Bristol as much as possible, within the framework of putting Trevor and the children first and yet to do so was proving impossible.

There were times when I felt I was being sucked under by a sea of pressure, resulting from divided loyalties and confusion. Could it be that something more insidious was going on of which I had been unaware? There was a constant ache in my heart for my mother, which never left me. Much as I loved her, I had become used to the fact that another personality would invade her being whenever the paranoia reared its ugly head. Even during the times when this was not apparent, we were subconsciously waiting in anticipation for the telling signs to appear, which in itself caused tension. This alien personality was incredibly powerful and controlling and also very believable. Sometimes it was so difficult to know to what extent to make allowances for her illness. It seemed to me that the margin between normality and abnormality was often blurred.

However much I may have tried to analyse what was happening, there was no escape from the fact that I did not feel free. There was a very strong pull towards Bristol and if I was perfectly honest, the whole situation had a hold over me in a way which was unhealthy and potentially quite destructive.

It would certainly suggest from the Scripture which Stanley had given me that God had taken me out of a manipulative environment into a new land, in order to set me free. I had never seen it that way before. There was no need to fear. His Holy Spirit was still with me and as the verse confirmed, remained with me. God was in control.

From the time that I received this Bible verse from Haggai, I began to try to trust God that He would take me back to Bristol, only under His direction and guidance. However strong the pull, however much I felt torn and the pressure was often great, I began to realise that in principle I should learn to wait until God opened the door. Then I would know that I was returning under His covering and protection. The same principle would also apply in terms of my mother's visits to our home in Ireland. Of course it is all very well to embrace a principle, but quite a different matter to have to put it into practice, as I was soon to learn.

6

HARRY AND AN ELDERLY AUNT

"In his heart a man plans his course, but the Lord determines his steps." (Proverbs16.9)

It seems to me that many of us have an elderly spinster aunt, whom over the years has become a firm favourite within the close family circle. For me it was my father's sister, known affectionate as 'Auntie Win.' She and her close friend Mollie had shared a home for many years and I loved them both dearly.

At the time when I received the phone call advising me of the car crash, they would have been in their late seventies. I do not know the details of the accident, but the result was that both ladies had been seriously injured and had been taken to Bristol Royal Infirmary. In time I learned that Auntie Win's injuries were much more serious than Mollie's and that they almost certainly contributed to her death some months later.

I was my aunt's next of kin and desperately wanted to travel to Bristol to be with her. Everything within me was screaming at me to board the next flight for Bristol and yet needless to say, it wasn't quite that simple. It seemed that yet again there were concerns about my mother's stability. She frequently came off her medication when she began to feel better, which made her very vulnerable and open to the illness invading her personality once more.

At times such as these, Trevor had made it abundantly clear that I was to stay away. He was not prepared to take any risks, especially in the light of the life threatening events some years previously. It would certainly be very difficult to travel to Bristol and not see or stay with my mother, who at that stage was managing to stay out of hospital and was living in a small flat on her own. Trevor's decision had been backed by the doctors involved, whose advice was to stay away when she was ill and to visit under their recommendation, either when she was in hospital or when she was stabilised.

Outwardly I had accepted this situation but inwardly, I kicked against it. Here again was a dilemma where I longed to go to Bristol and yet because of the obstacles, I was being prevented from doing so. In desperation, I rang Nancy, a close friend of mine who lived in Belfast; someone in whom I could trust to give me godly wisdom. Nancy would support me; she would understand, even if nobody else appeared to do so! Conscious of my frustration and anger at the whole situation and at just about everybody involved, I poured out my tale of woe to my good friend, who listened patiently, as I knew she would. Hoping that she would be able to conjure up some kind of ready-made solution to the whole scenario or "quick fix," I was a little disappointed when she simply said,

"Viv – when you put the phone down, I am going to pray for you and I want you to read Scripture. Ask God to speak to you directly through His Word. I am going to trust God for you that He will show you what to do."

Not wanting to let Nancy down and aware of her wise counsel, it was still with some degree of unwillingness that I thumbed through the pages of my "Daily Light" and found the reading for that particular day (April 6 evening). A verse which I had never ever heard or read before, leapt out of the page and took hold of me in a way that newspaper headlines seek to do on a daily basis but rarely succeed ....'Woe to those who go down to Egypt for help...." It was a line of Scripture which could so easily have been lost on the page, if God had not already spoken into my heart about the significance of Egypt. Looking up the context of the verse I read from Isaiah 31:1,

"Woe to those who go down to Egypt for help.....but do not look to the Holy One of Israel, or seek help from the Lord."

"Egypt, Egypt, Egypt." Here it was again. The words could not have been more specific or graphic. "Right Father," I said in my heart to God – "I will stop fighting you. I will not go to Bristol. I will wait for you to work out your purposes. But please, please, somehow, will you open up the way for me to go to Bristol soon, before it's too late?"

How did I explain my absence from a family crisis?

"Trust me Mum – trust me" was all I could say. Yet it was spoken with the quiet assurance that God really was at work on my behalf. Knowing that, gave me the freedom in my spirit to wait on Him to take me back to Bristol in His perfect timing. I am reminded of the verse, *"My soul, wait thou only upon God, for my expectation is from Him." Psalm 62:5 (King James.)*

Translated into my own situation I felt as if God was saying to me – "Do not fear my precious daughter. I know your heartache. I know your fears. Trust me. Take hold of my hand. Hear my voice saying to you – This is the way, walk in it and be at peace."

One of the people I contacted about my aunt's condition was my cousin Harry. He was actually a third cousin, but we were very close because there were so few relatives on my father's side. He lived near London with his wife and two daughters, so I didn't see them all that often. However, I knew how fond Harry was of Auntie Win as she was of him and that he would want to be made aware of her situation. A few days later he returned my call and spoke to Trevor, as I was out. Harry was planning to drive to Bristol the following weekend to visit her in hospital. Knowing the difficult circumstances regarding my family, he suggested that I flew to London. He would meet me, I would spend the weekend with his family, then he and I would travel to Bristol on the Saturday to visit Auntie Win together. I would be under Harry's protection and with him the whole time. Perfect solution! It certainly appeared as if God had answered my prayer.

I had become increasingly aware over the years that God often spoke to me through the Bible readings in "Daily Light." Undoubtedly, in the context of my present dilemma that had proved to be the case. So with some curiosity, I turned the pages of this little classic until I came to the date on which I would be travelling to Bristol with Harry (April 24th). I focused on one section included in the morning reading, taken from Gen.50.24, Acts 7.34,36 and Hebrews 10.23.

"But God will surely come to your aid and take you up out of this land to the land He promised on oath to Abraham, to Isaac and to Jacob...I have indeed seen the oppression of my people in Egypt. I have heard their groaning and have come down to set them free. Now come, I will send you back to Egypt...He led them out of Egypt and did wonders and miraculous signs in Egypt...He who promised is faithful."

Rarely had I known my heart to beat so fast! I could scarcely believe that God could, or would speak so directly into a situation, promising both protection and deliverance. It was a word from His heart directly to mine – a living, breathing, pulsating powerful word from God, which I could not, dare not deny. It was both humbling and thrilling at the same time. I wanted to shout from the roof tops how much my God cared for me and that *"...He is able to do immeasurably more than all we ask or imagine, according to His power at work within us...."* *(Ephesians 3:20.)*

This was of course the second time that God had spoken to me through Scripture in the space of a few days; the two passages being linked, because of the connection with Egypt. The latter, confirmed the former and also reaffirmed that God was going to guide me through what otherwise might have been a minefield of relationships. I should not have been surprised, but if I am honest, I did not expect God to step into my life quite so powerfully. My fragile faith dictates its own terms and limits my expectations.

Maybe, in a similar way, you have known God speak directly to you. When it happens, nothing else seems to matter. My God had spoken to me – my Father, whose heart was for me and who knew my confusion and my pain. He had visited me as clearly and as powerfully as if He had knocked on my door. I was learning that a word from God changes everything. It is a profoundly uplifting experience. It has the potential to free us from the shackles of the flesh and temporarily at any rate, makes us feel that like Peter, we too can walk on water. A word from our God, should in principle, take root and become part of the life within. It is that very word of God that has the power to renew the mind, in the way in which Paul describes in his letter to the Romans.

"Do not conform any longer to the pattern of this world, but be transformed by the renewing of your mind. Then you will be

able to test and approve what God's will is – His good, pleasing and perfect will. (Romans 12:2.)

Yet so often we miss the very word which God has for us. We may read it, but we do not receive it into our spirits. One of the most well known statements of Jesus is found in John 8:31-32

"If you hold to my teaching you are really my disciples. Then you will know the truth and the truth will set you free."

What is this truth of which he speaks? He of course is the truth (John 14:6). It therefore follows that His Word is also absolute truth. The two are synonymous. You cannot separate Jesus from His Word. To do so would be to compromise His integrity and question His relationship to His Father. It seems to me that there is a direct connection between the extent to which we receive biblical truth and the extent to which we are free. The one has a very real bearing on the other.

It is a constant challenge to receive God's Word on an ongoing basis. The Apostle Paul says in 1 Corinthians 13: 12:

"Now we see but a poor reflection, as in a mirror; then we shall see face to face. Now I know in part, then I shall know fully, even as I am fully known."

Very often we take on board only our perception of truth, which is coloured by the baggage we carry. It is filtered through our mindset, sifted like sand, subjected to our emotions and limited powers of reasoning. It is cushioned by an inbred desire to protect ourselves from anything alien which threatens our self-preservation… especially pain. Yet truth, however painful, is really the only thing which can set us free; truth which is encouraging, challenging and life changing, moving us constantly closer to the very heart of God and to that place of freedom and security which He offers us in Christ. Only then, can we become the men and women He created us to be.

Sometimes, just sometimes it seems to me, that God in His infinite compassion and grace will lift the veil from our eyes a little more and allow us a clearer vision of His purpose in our lives, so that we grasp something of His perspective and of His sovereign will.

The verses from "Daily Light" in connection with going to Bristol, was one of those times… and it was enough.

So it was with very little apprehension (except the thought of missing my flight, as I was on standby) that I drove to Aldergrove Airport, looking forward to a weekend with my cousin Harry and an opportunity to visit Auntie Win together; aware that I was travelling in God's timing and therefore ultimately under His protection. Needless to say, my visit to Bristol at that time was my last opportunity to see my aunt; she died a short while afterwards. But I moved through the weekend with a freedom and ease of knowing that it had been ordained of God. He had opened the door for me to go. His timing, as always, was perfect.

There is a huge sense of security in knowing that we are walking in the sovereign will of God. To my cost, I do not always find that place, let alone stay there. Yet it has certainly been my experience that on those occasions when I have finally given up fighting for my own rights, when I have finally said "Yes" to the Father Heart of God, somehow I am lifted to another plain. It is as if my whole being is in harmony with the will of God. At that moment there is a sense of release, of freedom and of intimacy with God, about which the world knows nothing, nor can it hope to compete. It is like breathing the purest air and bathing in the purest water and I know with a passion that cannot adequately be put into words, what Paul meant when he said,

"…Your life is now hidden with Christ in God." (Colossians 3.3)

7

LORNA AND THE IRONING

"To Him who is able to keep you from falling and to present you before His glorious presence without fault and with great joy...to the only God our Saviour be glory, majesty, power and authority, through Jesus Christ our Lord, before all ages, now and forever more! Amen." (Jude 24-25)

Having four small boys meant that the washing machine was constantly in use and that the ironing basket was never empty. In fact in those days, I had no idea what dim and distant item of clothing lurked at the bottom of the ironing basket, how long it had been lying there, or indeed whether it would fit any member of the family, assuming it was still in fashion. To ease the boredom of ironing, Lorna, a good friend and I, would meet each week and iron together, putting the world to rights as we did so and drinking our fair share of coffee in the process. One evening in particular, I remember driving home to Bangor from Newtownards, where Lorna lived. In the back of the family Ford

Estate was a large washing basket of neatly folded clothes, the result of a great evening's work, plus a rather precariously balanced ironing board. Lorna and I were very close friends. Our sons were about the same age and we had much in common. We had enjoyed a good time together that evening. Life was sweet.

Driving home, I started to praise God out loud for His many blessings and His continuing goodness to me. No one could hear me as I poured out my heart to God. I thanked Him for Trevor and my boys and then went through the usual gamut of blessings embracing good health, good lifestyle, great friends, great country and anything else which came to mind. As I carried on thanking God and praising Him, something totally unexpected and quite overwhelming happened. I am not given to hearing the audible voice of God, but I knew He was speaking to me. In my spirit I heard that still small voice saying – "But my child, my precious child, even before I blessed you, I loved you. I love you with an everlasting love…..You are mine…Learn to worship me for who I am first and foremost, not just for what I have given you…"

The impact these words were to have on me was immense. God was teaching me that in His goodness He blesses us and His blessings are a direct expression of His love for us. But sometimes, in His infinite wisdom and for His own purposes, He will withdraw a blessing from us and allow us to go through a dark place – and I had known more than one of those! Do I stop praising God at that point? Or do I hold fast to the truth that His love never wavers and that my security in this insecure world in which we live, is not to be found in any circumstances, be they favourable or unfavourable, but in the sovereign Almighty Father heart of God. How important is it to embrace the true character of God as revealed in His Son, in order to find our real identity and security.

If God were sovereign and yet not all loving, we would have no security. If He were all loving, yet not sovereign, we would be equally insecure. But within the framework of His sovereign love, we find total and complete security. A healthy relationship with God is not based on His blessings, but is rooted and grounded in Almighty God Himself. In this connection I find Oswald Chambers statement extremely challenging:

"Nothing is easier than getting into a right relationship with God, except when it is not really God you want, but only what He gives…" (My Utmost for His Highest)

Habakkuk understood this underlying truth when he wrote, *"Though the fig tree does not bud and there are no grapes on the vines, though the olive crop fails and the fields produce no food, though there are no sheep in the pen and no cattle in the stalls, yet I will rejoice in the Lord, I will be joyful in God my Saviour."(Habakkuk 3: 17-18)*

This is a basic Scriptural principle of which we are probably aware and yet I know for myself, that unless I constantly embrace its truth and apply it, my priorities become muddled. I am in danger of falling flat on my face at the first hurdle which threatens my home grown, fragile and inadequate sense of well-being.

8

CHRISTMAS AND THE SUPERMARKET

"He will cover you with His feathers and under His wings you will find refuge; His faithfulness will be your shield and rampart." (Psalm 91.4)

The inner struggles which confronted me regarding my mother's situation were put to one side periodically during times of great joy and fulfilment with Trevor and the boys. The nature of her illness was such that she could be well for months, even years and then the cycle would repeat itself and we would face another crisis.

During one such occasion, she had again been hospitalised in Bristol and I was in Ireland. It was Christmas 1989. How I longed to be with her. Yet again the doctors had advised against this. They had told me to stay in Ireland with Trevor and the children and they would call me if they felt I should go to Bristol. Although my mother had been asking for me, it was in the context of wanting to protect me from possible danger. The doctors had explained to me that to respond to her request would be to feed the paranoia and that it was wiser to stay away. Needless to say, I found this incredibly difficult and as had so often proved the case on past occasions, I felt very torn. I remember vividly the morning I parked the car at the local supermarket. It was a few days before Christmas and yet I felt no joy in my heart or desire to celebrate. I wept before God.

"Father" I cried, "I am so concerned about my mother – please show me what to do…."

I reached for my New Testament and Psalms, which at that stage I kept in my car. Turning the pages, my eyes focused on the last verse of Psalm 138, which in the King James Version begins with this statement,

"The Lord will perfect that which concerneth me…" I read the words several times and each time they became more meaningful. What had changed? Nothing in terms of my circumstances. My mother was still in hospital in Bristol and I was in Ireland. Yet I changed! I became aware that God was speaking to me through the Psalmist with a word which was so powerful in its implication, so full of potential and promise, so perfect in its timing, that I could not deny its truth, or the immediacy of its application. My Father had spoken to me. He had reassured me that He would sort out the circumstances which concerned me. I had only to trust Him and trust His timing, as the Psalmist had done hundreds of years previously and many countless troubled souls from that day to this. So I placed my hand back into His hand, received His Word into my spirit and moved forward, trusting Him to accomplish what I could not. Anguish began to give way to relief, relief to peace and peace to a freedom from the stress of being pulled in all directions.

Some weeks after this incident, when events were on a more even keel, my mother had recovered sufficiently to be able to visit us in Ireland and I knew that in God's timing, He had opened the door for that to happen.

However, Psalm 108: 8 became a verse to which I needed to return on more than one occasion and I discovered that the lesson it had taught me that day at the supermarket, was one which I constantly needed to relearn.

9

Thoughts About a Well-Worn Journal

"I believe in Christianity as I believe that the sun has risen, not only because I see it but because by it, I see everything else." C.S. Lewis.

Clearing out my desk recently, I came across an old student exercise book of mine which turned out to be a long forgotten journal. It was dated 1986 and I was aware that it hadn't been opened for many years. I promptly decided that the desk-tidying could wait; I made myself a cup of coffee, curled up in my favourite armchair and settled down to re-read some of my much earlier recorded thoughts. I have to say that I am not in the habit of writing a journal all of the time, although I know of many people who do so. I think it would be very helpful and certainly in times of crises, I have found it to be invaluable.

As I leafed through the exercise book, I saw that on the left hand pages, I had written the verses God had given me each day to challenge and encourage me. I smiled as I re-read my first entry, dated Dec. 20. 1986. In block letters, at the top of the left hand page, I had written,

"God will perfect that which concerneth me." Psalm 138.8 *(King James).* I glanced at the right hand pages. Here, I had listed the ways in which I could acknowledge God's hand on my life apart from relevant Scripture. In other words, I was learning to recognise His presence through everyday events. By this I mean a beautiful sunset, a visit from a valued friend, an encouraging phone-call, letter, or a particularly uplifting Sunday service. There were many more, but these are actual examples I had recorded and I noticed that every entry was dated. Both left and right hand pages revealed God's love for me and helped me in my search for a deeper communion with Him. Both pages spoke truth into my life and were extremely affirming and reassuring, even as I re-read them nearly twenty years later.

I wrote this journal during a particular season of my life, not because my faith was strong, but because my faith was weak and fragile; not because I constantly live the victorious Christian life, but because I easily feel vulnerable and defeated. I am prone to forget what God has said to me through His Word, unless I write it down and this in itself is a discipline. I know in principle that,

"In all these things we are more than conquerors through Him who loved us."(Romans 8; 37)

I also know that as believers,*"God has raised us up with Christ and has seated us with Him in the heavenly realms in Christ Jesus." (Eph. 2.6.)*

It follows that the believer's position is one of victory and authority in Christ and that never changes; it is constant and it is secure. It was won for us on our behalf by Christ at Calvary. However, when the evidence all around suggests otherwise, it is easy to fall prey to the enemy's lies. It seems to me that I am much more inclined to take on board a distortion of truth, based on the shifting sand of all that is going on around me, rather than embrace the uncompromising absolute truth of God's Word, which never changes. How much I need to counteract the negative with the positive and allow Scripture always to be my first point of reference.

I remember the first time I came across a passage in Revelation 12:10, 11.

"Then I heard a loud voice in heaven say, "Now have come the salvation and the power and the kingdom of our God and the authority of His Christ. For the accuser of our brothers, who accuses them before our God day and night, has been hurled down. They overcame him by the blood of the Lamb and the word of their testimony; they did not love their lives so much as to shrink from death."

It was as if a light went on when I read these words and realised just how powerful they were. The enemy may well continue to accuse (present tense). However, he has most emphatically been hurled down (past tense). He will use every trick in the book to render us less effective as Christians, even though he has already been totally defeated. All he can do as a result is lash his tail, like a snake that has already been shot dead. He has been overcome by the finished work of Calvary. Consequently, we stand with Christ, from this place of victory over the enemy who can never rob us of our position or of our God-given inheritance. That is the truth. It is the reality of our testimony and the triumph of the believer's life in Christ. There is of course, so much more to be gleaned from these verses in the book of Revelation, but in essence, that is the lesson I learnt from them.

I am such a slow learner and am happy so often to trust in my own limited ability to be in control under pressure, when all the resources of heaven are at my disposal, if only I would take advantage of them. Not only do I need to do so during times of difficulty, but also in the ordinary, humdrum activities of the day. Both areas are equally important to God. I am constantly learning new lessons about entering into the fullness of my inheritance in Christ and not just staying on the edge of all that He has done for me, timidly paddling on the shore when I could be venturing out into the deep and diving with dolphins.

The apostle Paul reminds us – *"No eye has seen, no ear has heard, no mind has conceived what God has prepared for those who love Him – but God has revealed it to us by His Spirit…"* *(I Corinthians 2: 9-10)*

All that God has prepared for us as believers, begins now of course and continues for all eternity. We can in this life, merely touch all that awaits us in heaven. Here we can simply taste something of the evidence of God's loving presence and look forward to the treasures which are in store for us in eternity.

As I studied this journal, I realised that all those years ago, I had begun to take on board the Scriptural principle which Paul writes about in Philippians 4: 8.

"Finally brothers, whatever is true, whatever is noble, whatever is right, whatever is pure, whatever is lovely, whatever is admirable, if anything is excellent or praiseworthy, think about such things." For me, that meant the discipline of waiting on God each day, focusing on Him to express His love and then writing down the ways in which He touched my life. During a particularly difficult time, this exercise became a life line.

In one sense, it was a form of cognitive behaviour therapy, which is so fashionable today and yet seems to me, to be totally biblical, if applied in the right way. It is a reminder yet again, of Paul's teaching on the renewal of the mind. Romans 12: 2 has already been quoted, but it is a verse which is absolutely crucial to our understanding of Christian principles and their application.

"Do not conform any longer to the pattern of this world, but be transformed by the renewing of your mind. Then you will be able to test and approve what God's will is. His good pleasing and perfect will."

One of the many areas involved in the whole process of renewing the mind (and the one which God had begun to reveal to me some years previously when I was at Cliff College) is to allow Christ to give us, *"a crown of beauty instead of ashes." (Isaiah ch. 61.3)* It is an exchange; His beauty for our ashes. The trouble is we want it both ways. We are by nature, a stubborn, self- absorbed race. We enjoy licking our wounds and feeding off our pain. I have heard Joyce Meyer, the well- known American Bible teacher state that although it is to our own detriment, we are so very often totally unwilling to give up our ashes and she's right isn't she?

10

CHOCOLATE CAKE AND AN UNTIMELY VISIT

"Fear not, for I have redeemed you; I have summoned you by name; you are mine. When you pass through the waters, I will be with you; and when you pass through the rivers, they will not sweep over you. When you walk through the fire, you will not be burned; the flames will not set you ablaze. For I am the Lord, your God, the Holy One of Israel, your Saviour."
(Isaiah 43.1-3a)

Trevor's brother Alvin and his wife Sandra have had many personal tragedies to bear, but they always have time for other people. They are both extremely caring and supportive. When the children were young, Alvin was an "Uncle Buck" character in their eyes and they adored him. They still do. He is warm, jovial and full of fun. None more so, than when he discovered Rob and Andrew, who were both at that time under five years of age, baking me a cake. It was 1981, Trevor had already left for work and I was heavily pregnant with David. I was finding it difficult to rouse myself and yet at about 7.30 in the morning, I was conscious that two little boys were in the kitchen and it was far too quiet!

"Mummy, Mummy," Andrew whispered, nudging me and forcing me to wake up. "We've baked you a cake. It's in the oven; come and see." Taking his hand and gingerly making my way to the kitchen, I was aware that I would probably need to brace myself for an appropriate response. However, nothing could have prepared me for the scene which met my eyes. Practically every work surface available was covered with flour, porridge oats, sugar, chocolate powder, salt, broken eggs and any other ingredient that the boys thought would add spice to their culinary efforts. Needless to say, the kitchen floor had also fallen victim to their well-intentioned plans.

My heart sank as Rob led me over to the cooker and proudly opened the oven door to reveal a large Tupperware bowl over laden with "gunge." Thankfully, I was in the habit of turning off appliances each evening, so there was no real danger, just an incredible mess! Unable to face clearing up everything and aware that reprimanding the boys was inappropriate, I sat them in front of their favourite cartoon video and steered myself towards the bathroom. Imagine my panic, when the doorbell rang! Grabbing my dressing gown, I peered behind the curtains to see Alvin standing there. He needed keys, which of course were in the kitchen. "Please don't look at the mess." I feebly pleaded with him, explaining what had happened. Rob and Andrew joined in, excitedly tugging at his sleeve and with that, a broad smile came over his face as he surveyed the scene.

Within half an hour he had returned, with something hidden under his jacket. Before the boys realised that he was back, Alvin had opened the oven door and exchanged their handiwork, for a large, fresh cream chocolate cake. To this day,

I shall not forget the cries of delight, as they beamed in wonder at their amazing success. Certainly, it was worth the massive clear up operation afterwards (or almost) just to witness the joy etched on their faces, as they tasted their "masterpiece" and happily shared it with Alvin and me. Delia Smith would have been proud of them.

So it was to Alvin that I turned some years later, when I received the phone call advising me that my mother had caught a flight to Belfast. I was aware that she was unwell and that she needed to be in hospital. However, she was not sufficiently ill to be sectioned and as was frequently the case, she was unwilling to be a voluntary patient. It was a scenario we had often faced. The normal arrangement was that she came to stay with us twice a year, subject to her taking her medication and with her doctor's approval. In terms of protecting the children and myself from any risk factor, Trevor had always said that if my mother ever flew to Ireland when she was in the middle of a breakdown, we would have to arrange for her to stay in a hotel. I hadn't argued with him, because I had hoped and prayed that it would never happen. But it did… and at a time when Trevor was away. He had taken his parents to Donegal for a few days and it was very unlikely that I would be able to contact him, or vice versa. It was before the days of mobile phones; he was touring and the telephone system in the Irish Republic was notoriously unreliable.

I was shaking when I lifted the phone and dialled Alvin's number and the tears came as I explained what had happened. How could I put my mother into a hotel? The words tumbled out as I heard Alvin's quiet, reassuring voice on the other end of the line saying, "If that's what Trevor has said must happen, that's what we must do." Having made hasty arrangements for the children, I drove to Belfast, collected Alvin and then we travelled together to the bus depot, where the airport coach would arrive. We guessed that was where we would find her, as she had not notified us of her plans, nor would she have arranged for anyone to meet her at the airport. We waited in silence, but the words inside my head were shouting at me, "Trevor doesn't understand. How can he expect you to put your own mother up in a hotel? How can you explain that to her? What kind of a daughter are you? What will people think of you? Are you going to reject her when she needs you more than ever? What do you think that will do to her?" Everything within me was reacting against what I knew I had to do.

Then I saw her. Alvin moved towards her, put his arm around her and gently guided her towards the car. She looked so vulnerable. I kissed her cheek and hugged her. But in my heart, I was weeping, searching for the right words, as she asked,

"Where are the children? May I see them?"

"Mum," I answered, still not sure how to reply and then as tenderly as I could, I found myself saying, "Mum, you're not well. The boys would be upset if they saw you like this. They would not understand. So we're not taking you home right now. We're going somewhere where we can have a cup of tea and you can have a rest and maybe see a doctor…"

"All right my dear, if you think so." She responded in a whisper. Alvin had already made initial enquiries about taking her to a hotel close to where he lived. Providentially, it happened to be the Glenmachan Hotel, which was run by a local church. We were greeted by warm and caring staff, who ushered us into a large lounge, overlooking Belfast Lough. As we were served afternoon tea, I studied my mother's face. She had not spoken since we had arrived at the hotel, but her eyes revealed so much to me. She seemed lost in a world light years away from reality and I sensed that I could not reach her. At last, a community psychiatric nurse arrived. She too, was unable to break through the wall of silence and eventually, my mother was admitted to Purdisburn Hospital, on the outskirts of Belfast, initially for a period of two weeks.

Driving home from the hospital several hours later, I desperately wanted to be able to contact Trevor. Alvin and I arrived back at his house, where Sandra had been looking after two of my boys, plus her own children. Whilst discussing the situation over a cup of tea, the telephone rang. It was Trevor.

"We're fine." I explained… "Except that my mother is here and Alvin and I have had to take her to hospital. But everything's under control now so don't worry about coming home…" Trevor's voice interrupted my feeble attempt to stay calm.

"I am home." He said, "I'm phoning from home. I came back earlier than planned and I have been wondering where you were. Stay at Alvin's. I'll be with you in half an hour."

Once Trevor arrived at his brother's house and I was able to put him in the picture, I relaxed a little. Amazingly, he had sensed that he needed to return home from Donegal, but did not want to disappoint his parents by cutting their holiday short. Having prayed that it would be possible to go back early if necessary, he was still somewhat surprised by his parents' reaction, later that afternoon. He had asked them, which part of Donegal they would like to visit the next day and quite unexpectedly, they expressed a wish to return to Belfast. This was totally out of character. Trevor's parents loved being with their children and especially holidaying with them. However, for whatever reason, they felt ready to return home, to the familiarity and comfort of their own surroundings… Who can doubt the wisdom and timing of Almighty God?

During the next two weeks I travelled from Bangor, through Belfast to Purdisburn Hospital, nearly every evening. The consultant caring for my mother proved to be extremely supportive. In fact, he arranged for Trevor and me to meet with him, during the time that she was being assessed. Referring to her file, he explained the nature of her illness. There was no cure and it was possible her condition would deteriorate, as she became older and more infirm. (Thankfully, this pattern did not emerge to the extent to which I had imagined.) He explained that there would be the same periods of normality, but that in all probability, the paranoia would return periodically and at varying degrees of severity. Medication, which at that time was a slow release injection every three weeks, would control the symptoms, but no more than that. He advised me that although he understood my need to support my mother in any way I could, it was important to be realistic. She was suffering from a chronic paranoid psychosis. It was a medical problem needing medical treatment. However much I longed to make her well, or lift her depression, I would never be able to do so. Realizing that I was becoming emotionally entrenched by events, he encouraged me to focus on my immediate family. He also explained that he was prepared to keep my mother under section, for a period of two weeks. During that time, medication which she had been neglecting to take in Bristol would stabilize her symptoms. Unless she was prepared to stay as a voluntary patient, he would have no alternative after the two weeks, but to release her.

I bombarded him with questions. She had already had more than one attempt at suicide and the overriding fear in me which began to surface again, was how much of a reality that might prove to be. I was struggling again not only with fear, but also with guilt. Why does guilt so often go hand in hand with fear? Both were unwelcome guests, having knocked on my door and forced an entry on more than one occasion. They were never in a hurry to leave and I was well aware that they were quite capable of taking up permanent residency, if I allowed them to do so, or gave them free rein. The one would feed off the other, bullying me into submission in the process. The guilt may well have been irrational and misplaced, but as so often in the past, I found it to be just as real and potentially, just as devastating.

I was too shaken to speak much on the journey home, except to ask Trevor if we could stop somewhere en route, for a cup of coffee and an opportunity to gather my thoughts. The consultant's advice could prove to be a two edged sword. He had made it very clear that I should not try to take full responsibility for my mother's condition. Yet to distance myself from her was so very painful and alien to the deep emotional ties which I felt so strongly as a daughter. The tragedy was that although my mother loved to come to stay with us, the experience sometimes unsettled her and tipped the balance of her fragile state of mind. She was frequently battling paranoia and her desire to protect those she loved would often surface when she was with them.

I remember over the next few weeks, being so much more aware of toddlers accompanied by their mothers and grandmothers on outings to the local park or to the shops. Would I be able to have a normal relationship with my mother again? Would my boys ever be able to enjoy a healthy, long term relationship with their grandmother?

The mother-child relationship is inevitably so deep. The umbilical cord may be severed at birth, but emotionally the tie can and often does remain. It seems to me that the life-blood can still flow from one to the other, in a way that is not always healthy or appropriate. Certainly, I had known a deep ache in my heart for my mother, which had never left me. If I allowed my concern for her to become all consuming, it followed that my ability to function as a wife and mother would be impaired. That had happened periodically and I guess it was at the core of what the consultant was saying. Wise words, but how to put them into practice?

Perhaps, you too have witnessed someone you love suffer deeply, either physically or mentally. You will understand the longing to put things right for that person, to make them well again and the feelings of utter helplessness and impotence at having to stand by, powerless. Putting her illness to one side, my mother was a wonderful person, with so much to give. She was warm, affectionate and wise. She was extremely intelligent, as I have already mentioned and she was very well read. She loved the Classics and would read the novels of Charles Dickens, Thomas Hardy and Jane Austen, over and over again, because she appreciated so much the authors' command of the English language and the beauty of their writings. What a tragedy that someone so gifted, as she surely was, should know from time to time, such darkness and torment. What a tragedy that anyone at all, should be visited by that kind of affliction.

At the end of two weeks, my mother discharged herself from the hospital, as I had expected she would. Her consultant had advised us to arrange for her to go back to Bristol, where her own G.P. would take over. So that is what we did. The family in Bristol (her sister and brothers) had been keeping in touch regarding events. All of them had been extremely supportive over the years and helped her in any way they could, especially her sister who was particularly long suffering. They were inevitably more involved than I was, except when she came to stay with us, because they lived in Bristol and were on hand should she need them. I shall always be grateful for the way they cared for her in so many practical ways. Family dynamics are never without their tensions and there were misunderstandings and differences of opinion from time to time. A senior social worker involved in her case, once told me that the nature of my mother's illness was tailor made to destroy families. Strong language, but I could see how the potential was there and I am so thankful that long-term, it was not the case.

Trevor and I always tried to make decisions based on what the doctors had advised, but of course it was extremely difficult attempting to satisfy everyone and I know that I failed in that area on more than one occasion. Happily, any conflict has been resolved and I enjoy a really good relationship with my family in Bristol, for more reasons than one, which will be explained later.

11

SONGBIRDS

"Sing, O Daughter of Zion; shout aloud O Israel! Be glad and rejoice with all your heart O Daughter of Jerusalem....The lord your God is with you, He is mighty to save. He will take great delight in you, He will quiet you with His love, He will rejoice over you with singing." (Zephaniah 3.14, 17)

Having witnessed so much depression in my immediate family, I remember crying out to God and asking Him that whatever came my way in terms of joy or pain, I would not have to know the utter blackness and despair which both my mother and sister experienced. I believe God graciously honoured that prayer and is still doing so to this day. I have known much sorrow in my life. I have known much pressure. But in this damaged, wounded world, that to a greater or lesser extent has simply been par for the course. Trusting God does not mean that we are immune from pain and I have met and read of many people whose journey through life has been far more difficult than mine. However, I shall be eternally grateful that I have been spared from suffering the kind of depression which for whatever reason, so many people have to bear in today's society.

Probably the Christian writer, from whom I have learnt the most, would be Oswald Chambers. His book of daily readings, "My Utmost for His Highest," has sustained me for many years. His words of wisdom, have nurtured me, encouraged me and challenged me practically every day since I was in my twenties. Frequently, I feel as though I am still only scraping the surface of all that this great man of God wants to teach me. A close friend of mine has shared with me that when she reaches heaven, she wants to find Simon of Cyrene and thank him for helping to carry Jesus' cross. I think that's a lovely thought, but when I reach heaven, I am going to make a beeline for Oswald Chambers, unless of course, I bump into Dietrich Bonhoeffer, C.S.Lewis, Henri Nouwen, or any other of the Godly writers who have inspired me over the years.

Turning the pages of this much loved devotional book, I studied the selected verse of Scripture for that particular day.

"What I tell you in the dark, speak in the daylight; what is whispered in your ear, proclaim from the roofs." (Matt10:27a) At that stage, this statement which Jesus made to His disciples, was not one that was familiar to me and yet the words "darkness" and "light," formed a connection in my thinking. To be honest, it is difficult to remember now whether the verse spoke directly to me because of a particular crisis, or simply because I was learning not only to recognise Scriptural principles, but also to appropriate them. The "dark" of which Jesus speaks in this verse, represented for me the place of pain and heartache. Yet here, Jesus is making it very clear that we must expect to find ourselves in such a position. He pre-

supposes that we will of necessity, find ourselves in the dark place:

"… In this world, you will have trouble…" (John 16: 33.) It is a foregone conclusion.

However, Jesus is also making it very clear that He is with us in the dark place, so close to us in fact that we would hear His voice speaking to us, if we would but listen! We might feel a sense of isolation and despair, but that does not negate the truth in any way. It simply means that the darkness can temporarily blind us from the truth. The reality of a beautiful sunset does not disappear, simply because we close our eyes to it. Whether we realise it or not, Jesus is with us in the darkness, standing alongside us. He never for one moment leaves us. Not only is He with us, but He is also teaching us, encouraging us in the darkness, exhorting us to hold onto the truth of His words until we are in the light. That is what is so wonderful about this verse and why it is so full of hope. We do not stay in the darkness. We move forward into the light. Jesus states categorically, that not only is He speaking to us in the dark place, but that He brings us out into the light, where we give testimony to all that we have learnt. It is good to be reminded that the darkness can never put out the light. Referring to this verse, Oswald Chambers comments that songbirds are taught to sing in the dark and that we are put in the shadow of God's hand, until we learn to hear Him…. *"When you are in the dark, listen and God will give you a very precious message for someone else, when you get into the light." (Oswald Chambers, "My Utmost for His Highest.")*

The psalmist David knew all about God's presence in the dark place and His promises to him, when he wrote these words… *"You, O Lord, keep my lamp burning. My God turns my darkness into light." (Psalm 18:28.)* David knew much about suffering, far more than I have ever known and yet in

Psalm 30.5 he was able to state with great conviction, *"…Weeping may remain for a night, but rejoicing comes in the morning."* So often in the Psalms it seems to me, that the writer moves with comparative speed from the "Why, Lord?" of questioning and doubt, to the "Yet will I praise you!" statement of trust. In reality of course, we have no idea of the time scale. It could well have taken the Psalmist weeks or even months to move from the painful honesty and confusion of his first position, to the security and freedom of worship, which the latter position allowed. Certainly, an act of will comes into play at some stage. In the same way, it probably took Habakkuk infinitely longer than we realise, to move from his stance before God of, "Why do the wicked prosper?" to his marvellous statement of faith, made in the last few verses of the book which bears his name and to which I have referred in a previous chapter. Thousands of years later, the human heart has not changed; I have come to realise in my own life that we can still find it just as difficult, but also just as necessary, to move forward, from a position of questioning God, to a position of trusting Him. However long that takes and however painful it proves to be, it is ultimately the only journey which can bring us to a place of resting and deep-rooted security. Then, like the Psalmist, we can also say,

"He who dwells in the shelter of the Most High
Will rest in the shadow of the Almighty.
I will say of the Lord, "He is my refuge
And my fortress, my God, in whom I trust." Psalm 91.1,2.

During the winter of 1984, when I was expecting our fourth son Richard, I had noticed another mother at church who was also pregnant. Margaret had two older sons and was now carrying her third child. She and her family lived close to us, although I did not know them well at that stage. However, I was aware that Margaret was a teacher. She was very capable and gifted, with a warm heart and a gentle spirit. Richard was a few months old when Margaret's son, David was born and it was a while before I heard that she was suffering from postnatal depression. More than fifteen years had passed, since my sister's illness and Margaret was the first person I had known since then, to be struggling with the same condition. The painful reality of my own experience surfaced and I sensed a strong compulsion to reach out to her. At the time leading up to Mary's death, I was only too aware that I was ill equipped to help her. I did not understand what was happening to my sister and I had absolutely no insight into the illness which was consuming her.

Today, as I type these words, I have in front of me two recently published articles on postnatal depression, each extremely informative and enlightening. Both articles explain how PND is different from "the baby blues." It is described as a slowing up; as impaired concentration; as profound feelings of unworthiness and guilt that the mother can't shake off .Her life has all the ingredients to be happy, but she feels an all pervading sadness. She has horrific morbid thoughts, perhaps about harming herself or her baby. I understand that the illness generally begins at about four to six weeks and gently gathers speed. It is considered to be due to a greater or lesser extent, to a hormonal imbalance. Apparently, the rarest form of PND is called puerperal psychosis (PP). This is when the mother experiences a break with reality and becomes deluded. Today of course, appropriate treatment is available, even for the most severe cases and the vast majority of mothers recover. I am sure Mary would have recovered too, given the resources available today. As it was, I believe she had no more control over her death than if she had suffered from terminal cancer.

In meeting Margaret, I was conscious of an enormous urge to be to her, what I had been unable to be, to my sister. I wanted to walk with her through the pain, darkness and confusion and to encourage her, that she could eventually be free from the clutches of depression. Thinking about my sister, I do not at any stage, remember feeling guilty that perhaps, I could have prevented her death in some way; just an overwhelming sense of sadness and loss which would consume me from time to time, although that did inevitably ease over the years. However, I do believe that my involvement with Margaret and the close bond we formed as a result of her illness was initially cathartic. I remember having a huge burden for her and constantly praying for her. I am absolutely sure God knew that psychologically, Margaret was someone I needed to encourage and He gave me a deep love and compassion for her. He also gave me the hope and assurance that she would be restored to full health and I believed totally that He was going to heal her.

Some years previously, when I was at an all time low, I had shared with a Canadian friend, that I felt too exhausted and weary, even to be able to pray. Laurie responded with these words "Don't try. I will pray for you, until you are strong enough to be able to do so again." I shall never forget the release I felt in my spirit, as I responded to Laurie's offer. Now, I wanted to do the same for Margaret, promising to intercede for her, until there was a real breakthrough in her life and despair had given way to hope. I had never before drawn alongside someone in that way and in one sense, it was uncharted waters. However, I felt able to share with Margaret that I believed she would recover, holding onto that truth for her, until she was able to believe it for herself.

During that time, an affinity developed between us which has deepened over the years and we have become like two sisters. I mentioned that the experience was initially cathartic, but it was so much more than that. Yet it was by no means a costly friendship. I never felt that I was being drained in spending time with Margaret, or in praying with her and there was a very real sense of anticipation, that all would eventually be well. What a joy it was therefore, to watch her gradual recovery and to see her take control of her life again. I must add of course, that I was not the only person on hand to help her. Margaret's husband, family and other close friends were extremely supportive, as was her doctor, who constantly monitored her medication and her progress.

Just recently, I asked her to describe something of those dark days to me. I also asked Sue, who had become my closest friend on the Isle of Man, how PND had affected her as a young mother some thirty years previously, after the birth of her second child. Both women had similar experiences; both spoke of their thinking becoming adrift when their babies were about six weeks old. Sue was convinced that there was something wrong with her baby. She became intensely over protective towards him and irrational, incapable of functioning beyond the boundaries of caring for him, even though she also had a four year old daughter. She was aware that she was spiralling downwards, but she felt powerless to stop that from happening. Guilt and failure consumed her; she was incapable of making any decisions and she was constantly exhausted. She didn't want to leave the house, not even to put the washing on the line. "It was like sliding into darkness." That was the way Sue described it. Margaret too, spoke of exhaustion brought on by sleepless nights, of a deep, deep all pervading sadness and a sense of utter despair. She could not even cope with the simple task of buying a loaf of bread and her husband had to bring her back from the local shop, in a state of panic. "I was locked into the darkness," she stated…..a similar description to the one used by Sue.

In the months and years after Margaret had recovered, we found ourselves drawn from time to time, to people who were struggling. For different reasons, we had both known the pain of being in a dark place and we had both known the joy of coming out into the light again. We were like two fledgling songbirds who, as Oswald Chambers described, had been put into the shadow of God's hand, so that we could learn to hear Him and then, testify to all that He had taught us. Our friendship became a springboard, as God began to put people in our path. Although inexperienced, Margaret and I together, tried to offer prayer support, encouragement and a renewed hope… Hope can become so fragile and illusive, once despair has beckoned, as I had discovered personally on several occasions.

Both Psalm 42 and Psalm 43 state these words….

"Why are you so downcast O my soul?
Why so disturbed within me?
Put your hope in God,
For I will yet praise Him,
My Saviour and my God."

Inspirational thoughts, hard to put into practice, but as already stressed, absolutely vital, even when it appears as if the whole world is against us!

12

A New Undertaking

"Carry each other's burdens and in this way you will fulfill the law of Christ." (Gal.6.2)

In time, I found myself involved in a pioneer work, which I believe was born out of my friendship with Margaret and our experiences of drawing alongside hurting people. It also arose from my involvement with the home group which Trevor and I had been running. At least three of the women who came to our home regularly, had suffered the anguish and pain of divorce. They had faced rejection in all its brutality and heartlessness. Rejection at its worst will attack the very core of our beings. It will scream at us that we are consigned to the scrapheap. We are of no value, worthless; we are failures. When Jennifer Rees-Larcombe's husband left her after many years of marriage, she said that she felt the word "Failure" had been written in red across her forehead. Constant rejection can move us to a place where we are extremely vulnerable. It can cause us to look for rejection where it does not exist; in fact, we come to expect it. We can become easily manipulated or even abused, all because of our desperate search for acceptance and validation.

I have heard it said that in the case of divorce, there are usually three sides; his side, her side and somewhere in the middle, the truth. That may well be correct, to a greater or lesser extent. Perception of truth, rather than truth itself, plays games with the mind and objective thinking becomes illusive. Every case is different of course, but whatever the circumstances and the reasons for a separation, there is inevitably a huge sense of loss and an overwhelming feeling of utter betrayal and abandonment by at least one party, if not both. The whole spectrum of emotion comes into play, with anger, guilt and an intense feeling of failure centre stage. It is a messy business; a weeping wound for so many members of the family, especially the children. There are no winners. Repercussions can drag on for years. Human nature plays the blame game; no one remains unscarred.

Aware that divorce was very much on the increase, a forward thinking Christian group which was called at that time, "Feminine Focus," arranged a springboard meeting in Belfast, to look at the possibility of setting up support groups. The aim was to offer encouragement and help to women who were going through the trauma of separation or divorce. "Feminine Focus" has more recently been renamed "Focusfest." It is a branch of "Evangelical Ministries," based in Northern Ireland. The vision of "Focusfest" is to help women discover their potential and release their gifting within their local church and beyond. This springboard meeting took place around 1987. I went along with the three women I mentioned from our home group, plus another friend who was recently divorced.

We were absolutely amazed by the response. Far more women were present than we had anticipated. In fact, the room was packed. Three women were interviewed and asked to describe the devastating effect that their marriage break-ups had caused them. They were all painfully honest. A tangible wave of understanding and empathy swept over the crowded room, as countless hurting women identified with their plight and visibly responded. Resulting from that meeting, several support groups, called "Rebuilders," were set up across the Province. These groups were not in competition with "Relate." In fact, their role was quite different. Nor were they seeking to make a doctrinal statement about divorce. They were simply trying to follow the example of Jesus and show compassion to hurting people. With "Rebuilders," that meant helping women pick up the pieces of their lives, after their marriages had irretrievably broken down.

Each group had two leaders; one who had been through separation or divorce and the other, who had a healthy stable marriage relationship and who was there mainly to keep a balance in the group. That's where I came in. I am aware of course, that sometimes it is the wife who betrays her husband and he is the one left to cope with the aftermath. When that happens, certainly he needs just as much support, but my experience was always with the women.

I look back now, on the years that I was involved with "Rebuilders" and count it an absolute privilege to have known so many immensely courageous women, who, although raw from dealing with the reality of rejection, were determined not to let their circumstances destroy them. Some have remained close friends and over time, we have laughed and cried together on many occasions.

Henri Nouwen writes, *"When we honestly ask ourselves which people mean the most to us, we often find that it is those who instead of giving advice, solutions or cures, have chosen rather to share our pain and touch our wounds with a warm and tender hand. The friend who can be silent with us in a moment of despair or confusion, who can stay with us in an hour of grief or bereavement, who can tolerate not knowing, not curing, not healing and face with us the reality of our powerlessness, that is a friend who cares."*

Within the groups, I felt very much that my role was primarily one of listening. The members themselves were very good at encouraging each other, especially those who were further along the road to recovery. They would inspire newer, more vulnerable members, whose wounds had not yet begun to heal. They affirmed their pain and gave them a very real sense of hope that in time, they would become stronger and would be able to take control of their lives again. They helped the new members to face their fears, believe in themselves once more and regain their sense of self- worth, always within the setting of a safe place, where they had learnt to trust and totally accept one another. As for myself, I was aware that I did not have the same degree of credibility, because I had not walked that particular path. I watched and listened and "chipped in," when it seemed appropriate, seeking to steer the meetings in the right direction. It was a learning curve for all of us. I felt their heartache as together, within the group, we focused on Scripture which specifically helped the members to deal with negative thoughts…We prayed, we drew exceptionally close and we constantly trusted God for healing.

Eleanor Roosevelt once said, *"It is a curious thing in human experience, but to live through a period of stress and sorrow with another person, creates a bond nothing seems able to break."*

I am so conscious that the Father Heart of God longs to embrace the hurting and the forsaken. From before the time that God pursued a frightened, abused and rejected Hagar, in the desert of Beersheba (Genesis 16) providing for her and for her son Ishmael, this same loving God has been reaching out to broken lives. Nothing has really changed since then. God is still God and pain is still pain.

You may have heard the quotation "Any work done for God, must be done by God." How true that is. "Rebuilders" has more recently been called "Divorce Care," which is the name of the resource material now used by each support group, but it must essentially be a work of God. His Son has drunk the bitter cup of rejection. He alone fully understands sorrow and is acquainted with grief. He alone can bring healing.

So it is the life of Christ within us that must be released in a way that makes a difference in our world, because He is the source of all deliverance, healing, wholeness, freedom and peace.

People who are bleeding inside and feel abandoned need to know that the one who ultimately understands their pain is the very one who has promised, *"....Never will I leave you, never will I forsake you."(Hebrews 13: 5)*

The Lord truly is our shepherd…. He makes us lie down in green pastures… He leads us besides quiet waters….

And in His infinite timing, compassion and grace, He is the one, the only one, who can totally restore the soul.

13

ROLE PLAY

"Spread the corner of your garment over me……."
(Ruth 3.9)

"Before God I will make the decisions on your behalf regarding your mother and before God, I will take the consequences."

I had not expected Trevor to make that statement; it came as a total surprise, especially as he said it with such conviction and authority. He is not very tall, but right then in my eyes, he rose in stature and he became at least six foot six. It was almost as if God was saying to me, "What have I got to do to show you that I have given you a man whose yes means yes and his no means no; a man who has your best interests at heart and who will make wise decisions when you are unable to do so?"

Again we had hit a difficult patch with my mother and yet again I was in turmoil about the best way forward. We had been discussing the situation until we were both tense and frustrated and I was feeling the full weight of the crisis on my shoulders. Did Trevor really understand? How could he? She was my mother, so it seemed to me that I should know what was best for her, not he. We were both involved and I appreciated his support, but I had always felt that I was the one who was responsible for her. However, here I was, buckling under the strain of it and becoming so emotionally worn out that I was incapable of making any rational judgement.

"I said before God I will make the decisions......." Trevor began to repeat himself, but I had heard him the first time. At that moment, I was conscious that the heavy burden was being lifted off my shoulders and that Trevor was now carrying it. It didn't seem to crush him like it had been crushing me; in fact, he seemed to want to take it on board. What had happened?

John Bevere, an American writer and Bible teacher, wrote a book a few years ago called "Under Cover," in which there is a section on the role of the husband in marriage and the role of the wife. He states that leadership in the home is given by God to the husband, not to the wife. He goes on to say that for the wife, it is a heavy yoke, but for the husband, it is a mantle and that God gives the husband the grace and the anointing to carry it. That makes sense to me and it is certainly in line with the apostle Paul's teaching about marriage in Eph.5.22-33. I believe that where the role play in marriage is acted out within the context of Scriptural principles, assuming both partners are in good health, husband and wife dove-tail together and the relationship between them is not only very beautiful, it is also very powerful and very freeing for both of them. The tragedy, as we see so often, is that these principles are frequently misinterpreted and consequently abused.

I love the story of Ruth and Boaz and how he became her kinsman redeemer. Boaz was Ruth's covering, her protector and her provider; well able to give her the security she needed. He was strong and steadfast, loyal and true; a real man, with a heart for God and a deep love and respect for Ruth. Wow! I think that most women are looking for modern day versions of Boaz. I would hate to be married to a man who leaned on me all the time and who was so weak that he expected me to make all the decisions. I'm aware that I can't expect to have it both ways. It would be nice to be able to dictate my own terms when it suited me, but it is far more important for me to have the reassurance that when necessary, my man will make a wise decision which is in my best interests and that he is prepared to carry the weight of responsibility that goes along with it.

My marriage to Trevor has always been fairly traditional. We have traditional roles, with Trevor being the sole bread winner once the children arrived. I am happy with that arrangement and we are fortunate that his salary provided a comfortable, but not extravagant life style. We respect each other's role, work as a team and play off each other's strengths. Certainly there were issues we needed to work through together, especially in the early years and it is not always easy. However good a marriage is, it is still imperfect and ours is no exception. We get it wrong sometimes. But we want to get it right more often and I guess that helps.

The day that Trevor made the statement I have referred to here, is a day when I believe we got it right. He took the initiative and I trusted him to be in control of the situation which was crushing me and making me feel so vulnerable. I let him carry the weight of it. He invited me to do so. In fact, it is important to state that I trusted him not only with the responsibility of the immediate crisis, but as far as I was able, with the long term situation. As an act of will, I handed over the reins. You could say that I gave him his place. It was, as John Bevere had said, a heavy yoke for me but a mantle for Trevor. In a healthy God given way, I submitted to Trevor's loving leadership and slotted in beside him. Within that framework, I experienced his covering and his protection, which was such a relief, as he took the lead, and hand in hand we faced the crisis together.

I wonder what Ruth would have thought.

14

DAVID AND AN IMPORTANT QUESTION ANSWERED

"Your word is a lamp to my feet and a light for my path."
(Psalm 119.105)

My son David had gone to bed at his usual time that night. It was 1993, he was twelve years old and he was allowed to read for a while before going to sleep. Like his brothers, he had also been encouraged to read a few verses from his Youth Bible each night, using Bible study notes for his age group as a guide. I remember going into his bedroom to spend a few minutes with him, before turning off his light. Seeing that he was reading a comic, I wondered if he had opened his Bible at all that evening. On further investigation, he explained that he wasn't sure if he wanted to pray, or read any Bible verses. He couldn't see God; how could he be sure that He was really there? What was the point? How could he believe in a God who was invisible, or speak to someone he couldn't see? I sat on his bed and we talked. What could I say that would be real and absolutely relevant for him? I answered his questions as best I could, aware that he was genuinely struggling and that the honesty of his questioning was a healthy sign of a son who was maturing and thinking things through for himself.

After a while, I suggested that we turned to his Bible study notes and the short reading for that evening. It turned out to be just one verse, where Jesus was addressing His followers.

"But when you pray, go into your room, close the door and pray to your Father, who is unseen. Then your Father, who sees what is done in secret, will reward you." (Matthew 6.6.)

It was a verse which I had read many times before, but never with such significance. My son, however, was not familiar with the verse.

"Listen to this, David!" I exclaimed in amazement and I read him the Scripture, as if I had triumphantly solved the last clue in the "Sunday Times" cryptic crossword.

"You're making that up!" He replied. Reading the verse for himself, he was silent for a moment. In fact, we both were, for I was very aware that God was speaking to him. It was as if God had leaned out of heaven and tenderly whispered a word from His heart to David's heart, to encourage and affirm him, exactly when it was most needed. It could not have been more timely. That the God of all creation could be so concerned about a twelve year old boy and his questions just overwhelmed me. As a mother, it was a huge encouragement for me as well as for David and a reminder that God understands our difficulties and our struggles. He is a Father who cares passionately about His children. Matthew 6.6. became a verse which lived in my son's heart for a very long time and he fell asleep that night, secure in the reality of God's love for him and also, reassured that it was all right to ask questions.

Why do I share this story with you? It is because I think we are very like David. If we are honest with ourselves, there are times when we ask similar questions. At least, I know I do… "Where are you Lord? I've lost sight of you. I'm in a dark place. How do I know that you're with me? Why haven't you answered my prayers? Do you not care? Have you abandoned me? Perhaps you're not there at all." Truth can so easily become distorted when we're passing through a valley and we allow negative feelings to reign supreme, invading our security in God. We are in good company, because we can certainly identify with the Psalmist and his honesty, in sometimes questioning God's apparent indifference to his predicament. However, our circumstances are of course notoriously unreliable, in terms of seeking evidence of God's faithfulness and of the reality of His love for us. My son David was not encouraged by a change in his situation, although he had the same struggles as most youngsters growing up and no doubt he had prayed that God would make things easier for him. It was a direct Word from God Himself which really made the difference. *Psalm 119 v. 130 states,*

"The unfolding of your words gives light; it gives understanding to the simple." How true that is for us as we read Scripture and how reassuring, that the God who recognises our deepest needs, will whisper a Word in season from His heart to our hearts, whenever we are willing to receive it.

15

LOVE BY PROXY

"True friends do not spend time gazing into each other's eyes.
They may show great tenderness towards each other, but they
face in the same direction…towards common projects,
goals…above all, towards a common Lord."
C.S.Lewis.

Let me tell you about Peggy. She was an elderly lady who came into our lives many years ago when we were living in Bangor, Northern Ireland. She just telephoned us one day and I cannot honestly remember how she knew of us. As far as I can recall, it was something to do with her sister, who lived in England and I think she had given Peggy our phone number. How she knew the number is a mystery, because at that time, we were ex-directory. Through the love and support of friends, Peggy became a Christian and although her life was far from easy, she was totally committed to her new found faith. She became involved in her local Presbyterian church and she came regularly to the Monday night meetings in our home. In her younger days, Peggy had been a professional cook and her baking skills were quite amazing. She could still make the best apple tart in Northern Ireland, with the pastry on top artistically latticed and glazed to perfection. We could tell when she arrived for our meetings, whether Peggy had been baking that day. She would be sporting a broad smile and carrying a small tray over which a check tea- towel had been carefully placed. We knew how to react when she ceremoniously lifted the tea- towel. Our praise and admiration for her handiwork were genuine. She was conscious of that and she loved it, aware that we were all looking forward to apple pie and cream later in the evening. I was always given strict instructions as to how long to re-heat the pie in my oven and woe betide me if I did not carry out those instructions correctly. Somehow she always knew!

Peggy was not an easy person. She could be quite cantankerous and she was very much set in her ways. She was a Yorkshire woman and as such, would call a spade a spade. In fact she was extremely blunt and at times could cause offence quite easily. But underneath her abrasive manner was a deeply wounded soul and a very lonely person, who had been dealt more than her fair share of heavy blows during her difficult life. I have to confess that I was not immediately drawn to her. She was slightly intimidating and she could be extremely intolerant. But for whatever reason, we seemed to spend an increasing amount of time in each other's company and I grew to love her very much, often smiling at her foibles. I can picture her now, putting on her gloves and then placing her handbag on her lap and closing it most emphatically, so that the clasp snapped in a way which attracted everyone's attention. As far as Peggy was concerned, that heralded the end of the meeting. She had had enough and she was ready to go home.

As Peggy and I came to value each other more and more, it dawned on me one day that she was exactly the same age as my mother. They had been born within a few months of each other. Although they were certainly very different in personality, temperament and background, they had both known a great deal of pain in their lives. Was God teaching me an important truth here? Since moving to Northern Ireland, there had been this constant frustration of not being able to channel my love for my mother in practical ways, on an on going basis. Was God showing me that all this pent-up love could be expressed to Peggy instead? A kind of love by proxy, if you like. If this was true, then maybe I needed to trust God more in terms of knowing that He would take care of my mother, whilst I helped to care for Peggy. Perhaps it really was that simple and in effect He was saying to me, "You concentrate on Peggy and I'll concentrate on your Mum." Could He make sure that people who loved my mother would support her and be there for her, when I could not do so? Could I really count on God to do that? I remember the very first time I realised this was a distinct possibility and it was very comforting. He is omnipresent after all, so it should be no problem for Him to be available in two places at once. Over the years since then, God has most certainly been faithful. The very real fears I had concerning my mother's condition were never fully realised and He did set in place friends and family who loved her and supported her. In retrospect, I do believe that God brought Peggy into my life, perhaps more for my benefit than for hers. The friendship certainly fed a need in me at that particular time.

About eight years ago, I received a telephone call from a mutual friend, who told me that Peggy was in a nursing home, suffering from cancer. By that stage, Trevor and I had moved to the Isle of Man with our sons. I had not seen my friend for some time and had not known of her ill health. But before Peggy died,

I was able to visit her in the nursing home in Ireland, just once. She opened her eyes and smiled at me. We said very little. We had no need to, but our reunion was very timely and so very precious.

I'm not sure how much the seed of faith was nurtured in me through this episode in my life. Looking back, I am conscious that yet again, God had created an arena where by I could move to a position of trusting in Him to work out His purposes. Staying focused on that is not always easy of course. However, I remember my friend Peggy with a very real affection and an awareness that the relationship was not only special, but also I believe, extremely significant for both of us. She would not have been conscious of it, but she blessed me and she enriched my life. For that reason, if for no other, I do not regret one moment of the time I spent with her and I like to think that our friendship brought joy to God's heart too.

16

A Man in Crisis

*"Moses heard the people of every family wailing, each at the
entrance to his tent. The Lord became exceedingly angry and
Moses was troubled. He asked the Lord, "Why have you
brought this trouble on your servant? What have I done to
displease you that you put the burden of all these people on
me? Did I conceive all these people? Did I give them birth?
Why do you tell me to carry them in my arms as a nurse
carries an infant, to the land you promised on oath to their
forefathers? Where can I get meat for all these people? They
keep wailing to me "Give us meat to eat!" I cannot carry all
these people by myself; the burden is too heavy for me. If this
is how you are going to treat me, put me to death right now…if
I have found favour in your eyes and do not let me face my
own ruin."
The Lord said to Moses "Bring me seventy of Israel's elders
who are known to you as leaders and officials among the
people. Have them come to the tent of the meeting that they*

*may stand there with you. I will come down and speak with
you there and I will take of the Spirit that is on you and put the
Spirit on them. They will help you carry the burden of the
people, so that you will not have to carry it alone."*
Numbers ch. 11:10-17.

One of the advantages of writing this book is that I can share
with you my all-time favourite Bible passages; passages which
have proved to be hugely significant for me over the course of
time, colouring my thinking and changing my perspective on
life. Numbers: ch. 11 is one of them, because it illustrates so
vividly the basic human need for companionship. I'm sure much
has been written about these powerful verses and Bible scholars
have no doubt added weight and relevance to their meaning.
But doesn't Moses' predicament speak to all of us? Here is a
man, chosen by God to fulfil an immensely significant role and
equipped by God to accomplish that role. Yet here is this same
man, battered and bruised and overwhelmed by the enormity of
the task assigned to him. We find him consumed with self pity,
anger, frustration, loneliness and exhaustion. I want to embrace
the painful honesty of Moses, as he bears his soul before God
and blames his Creator for his plight. It is not difficult to
empathise with his vulnerability, his despair and his sense of
rejection. Having to face yet another day, being crushed by such
a heavy burden was just too much for him and he wanted to
escape. Sounds familiar? It is kind of typical of our defeatist
attitude isn't it? How often in my own life have I complained to
God that the cares, the responsibilities and the dilemmas I face
(for less reason than Moses) are just too much to carry? Ever
wanted to escape? If so, you're in good company.

In my experience, the journey along the road called "Self
Pity" has turned out to be a cul-de sac every time and at some
stage I have had to turn back. The alternative would have been

to stay put, dig a trench and make licking my wounds a life time habit. However, the one who created me and who knows my tendency to become self absorbed at the first opportunity, is also the one who can lift me above my frailty and my sense of impotence.

So how does God handle this bewildered, misunderstood servant of His? Not with condemnation that's for sure. Nor does He strike Moses dead on the spot and so grant him his wish. God's reply embraces understanding and compassion and He is just so patient. His answer is to give Moses something to do which is well within his capabilities, but which will take his mind off himself and also encourage him that all is not lost. Moses simply had to bring the seventy leaders to the appointed place, the Tabernacle, at the appointed time. God did the rest, as He had promised. He did it in response to His servant's anguish, so that Moses would not have to carry the weight of responsibility and the burden of the people *all on his own.*

I love this story because it demonstrates God's heart. The reality, in this broken bleeding world in which we live, is that there will be times when we struggle. However, God never intends you or me to be in pain or to struggle alone. We only have to look at Scripture to find many examples of true friendship. For King David, there was Jonathan and in that beautiful statement in 1. Sam.18:1 (King James) the depth of their relationship is described.

"…..the *soul of Jonathan was knit with the soul of David, and Jonathan loved him as his own soul.*"

In the New Testament, we read that Jesus sent His disciples out in twos and He Himself, chose twelve friends of whom three, shared a special closeness with Him.

We were created for community. In John Ortberg's book, "Everybody's Normal Till You Get to Know Them." The author discusses God's marvellous statement in the Garden of Eden, "*It is not good for Man to dwell alone."* He explains that the statement was made before the Fall and that even when Adam was in perfect harmony with his creator, God was aware that it was not enough. His work was not complete. Adam needed companionship. He needed a soul mate…and God created Eve. God blessed them and said to them,

"Be fruitful and multiply…" (Gen.1.28a). From that union, community was born and family life began.

On the theme of community, the well-known Christian psychologist, counsellor and author Dr. Larry Crabb, made this statement…

"The greatest need in modern civilization is the development of communities…true communities where the heart of God is at home, where the humble and wise learn to shepherd those on the path behind them, where trusting strugglers lock arms with others as together they journey on." (From "Connecting.")

It seems to me that we speak of the Body of Christ from our perspective, as a New Testament term and of course it is, in that all believers are part of His Body. However, from God's perspective, the concept was essentially birthed in His heart from the beginning of time. We are the Family of God and we need one another. Pride dictates its own terms and for some, it is harder to accept this need than it is for others. But once we become believers, we are inextricably bound together by the love of the Father and the life of Christ within us. We are a fellowship…the fellowship of all believers and being part of God's family has certainly been incredibly important to me over the years.

In his book "Life Together." Dietrich Bonhoeffer writes in a similar vein to Dr. Larry Crabb...

"Christian brotherhood is not an ideal which we must realize; it is rather a reality created by God in Christ, in which we may participate. The more clearly we learn to recognise that

the ground and strength and promise of all our fellowship is in Jesus Christ, the more serenely shall we think of our fellowship and pray and hope for it."

Of course there are times when I have just needed to pick myself up and get on with it, but there are also many occasions when a kind word, a shoulder to lean on or a listening ear is not only exactly what I have needed, but it has also been providential. I think it was Henry Drummond who once said that there was no greater thing we could do for our Heavenly Father than to be kind to one of His children. Where does this kindness come from? In its purest form, it springs from God Himself and it is expressed through His Holy Spirit within us. How many times have I been on the receiving end of this kind of encouragement and blessing! There have also been times when I have needed the appropriate person to challenge me and keep me on track. Accountability is very healthy and very important, so that we are less likely to stray outside our God-given boundaries, become vulnerable and fall prey to the enemy. But whatever the situation, God seems to go out of His way to set in place the right people who are there, just when I have needed them. Why would He do that if it weren't for the fact that He understands our needs? He is sovereign and He is faithful to His promises that He will provide and care for us.

This brings us back to Moses…. God did not ask Moses to find seventy elders who would support their leader in their own strength. They were not expected to fulfil their task under their own steam, any more than Moses was. In *Numbers ch. 11 v. 17, God says, "…I will take of the Spirit that is on you and put the Spirit on them. They will help you carry the burden of the people so that you will not have to carry it alone."* God not only equipped Moses with seventy people to support him, but also gave them the resources to help. In so doing, Moses was able to re-focus and his hope was renewed. The resources are needless to say, rooted in the Holy Spirit, for it is only through God's Spirit that the believer is truly in a position to offer effective support.

Of course the number of elders in this story is not what really matters, at least not in terms of what we can learn from it. But it is extremely important that they stood *with* Moses, along side him, presenting a united front and empowered by the Spirit of God to encourage and support him. In my experience, that has always been the greatest antidote to despair.

"Not by might, nor by power, but by my Spirit, says the Lord Almighty." Zechariah 4:6.

If I were to introduce you to some of my "seventy elders," they would be people who have seasoned my life with warmth, humour, wisdom and love and who have allowed me to lean on them a little, when I have needed to do so. They may not have been "leaders and officials" in the biblical sense, but they have all demonstrated God's love to me and the presence of His Spirit in their lives. Sometimes, the support has come from being part of a close- knit, church based fellowship or prayer group, where friendships have been nurtured in a safe environment, because unconditional acceptance and trust is fundamental to the group. That kind of honest reality takes time of course and masks are removed gradually. Equally, individual friends have played their part. Many reached out to my mother, when she came to stay with us, loving her and welcoming her into their homes, helping her to feel valued and accepted. I appreciated their kindness so much. I have already mentioned Laurie, who carried me in prayer for a while and Nancy who spoke truth into my life when I needed to hear it. An American friend fasted and prayed for a whole week on behalf of one of my sons, who at eighteen years of age, was in danger of completely losing his way. (I would not have known about her intercession, if her daughter had not told me at a later date.)

Imagine making that kind of sacrifice for someone else's child!

Then there was Beth... At the time that we lived in Bangor, she was a neighbour of mine and a good friend, who was brilliant at baking, just like Peggy. She arrived on my doorstep one day carrying the most enormous quiche I have ever seen; large enough to feed an army. She had heard that we had visitors staying with us and she thought the quiche might help. It certainly did. I was at the back of the queue when cooking skills were given out, so any contributions are always readily accepted, especially when we have guests. To be honest, I have never been that keen on spending hours in the kitchen, stirring pots and pans, trying to keep everything hot until the last minute and rolling out pastry at the same time. It has never quite worked for me like that; nor have I ever been any good at following recipes. There is usually at least one ingredient that I've never heard of, so I either give up there and then, or improvise, with disastrous results. Thankfully, Trevor has become used to my humble efforts and has always been very accepting. I can do an excellent Sunday lunch and my cottage pie is not bad, but anything fancy or remotely exotic doesn't stand a chance in my kitchen.

On that particular occasion, we were looking after a missionary family from Canada for a short while. When they arrived, I had asked the husband what area of work he had been involved in before becoming a missionary, only to be told that for several years, he had been head chef at a top hotel in Canada! What a joke… my attempt at being the perfect hostess was not exactly boosted at that point and I could see my 'street cred.' disappearing out the window. "Can't fool this guy," I thought, continuing to smile politely at him, although panic was quickly setting in, aware that he could probably smell Marks and Spencer's pre-cooked meals a mile away. The children were still young and really, in retrospect it was all too much, with nine people to feed every day. Looking back, perhaps we should have changed roles and he could have done the cooking…not a chance! I remember being very tired one afternoon, having run out of ideas for meals and wondering if I could get away with cottage pie again that evening. Perhaps I could disguise it in some way. If not, it would most likely be a burnt offering… when Beth suddenly called. At that moment, she became my angel sent from heaven.

It is a long time ago since this episode happened and in the scheme of things, it was just a small incident. I expect she has forgotten all about it; but I have not forgotten and I'm quite sure that God remembers too. He tells us so in Hebrews 6.v.10.

"God is not unjust; He will not forget your work and the love you have shown Him as you have helped His people and continue to help them."

How encouraging for us… and freeing too, knowing that whether we are helping others, or receiving help ourselves, it is ultimately about expressing the reality of Christ's love, through the power of His Holy Spirit. In so doing, we are serving the God who cares intimately about us. We are also I believe, functioning within the Body of Christ in the way that He intended and therefore, beginning to reflect something of His image.

A while ago, I listened to a story which I found incredibly challenging….

"A man called Joe had been miraculously converted. God had met with him in a powerful way and he had given his life to Christ. Prior to that, Joe had the reputation of being a drunk, for whom there was no hope…only a miserable existence wandering the streets, with nowhere to live. Following his conversion to a new life in Christ, everything changed. Joe became the most caring person that anyone associated with the local mission had ever known. He would hang about the place,

doing whatever needed to be done. Nothing was beneath him. He would clear up vomit. He would scrub the toilets. He would do so with a smile on his face, grateful for the chance to help. He could be counted on to feed feeble men, who wandered into the mission off the streets. He would undress and tuck into bed, men who were too "out of it" to take care of themselves.

One evening, the director of the mission was delivering his message to the usual crowd of still silent men, with drooped heads. Suddenly, one man looked up. He came down the aisle to the altar and knelt to pray, crying out to God to help him change. The repentant man kept shouting, "Oh God...make me like Joe...make me like Joe!" The director leaned over and said very gently to him "Son, I think it would be better if you prayed, make me like Jesus; make me like Jesus." The man looked at him puzzled and with tears in his eyes asked,

"This Jesus....is he like Joe...is he like Joe?"

17

A Time for Confrontation

"... You will know the truth and the truth will set you free."
(John: 8.32.)

It was December, 1994. I had been sitting in the lounge on my own for quite a long time, staring at a lukewarm cup of coffee. No one else was in the house. The boys were at school and Trevor was at work. Within the next few days, my mother would be coming to stay for three weeks over the Christmas period and I was dreading it. I do not recall that she was particularly ill at the time, but I had reached the stage when I was apprehensive about any impending visit. There always seemed to be a shadow around her, which was not her fault, although for me it was a constant reminder of the heartache we had both experienced and I was weary of it. I longed to move on and leave the past behind. However, whenever we were together it seemed that I had to face it yet again. She looked forward to her visits so much and it was right that she came to stay, especially at Christmas; but I wanted to run away. Conscious of my fear, of my resentment and of my totally self-absorbed attitude, I had gone into the lounge that morning to wrestle with the problem and hopefully resolve it in some way.

It was of course so much easier for me to move on. The arena of pain had been Bristol. My life was now based in Ireland and my focus was very much Trevor and the boys. I wanted to look forward, not backwards. But for my mother, it was much more difficult. Most of her years were behind her and I sensed that there was something of her wanting to live out her remaining years through me. At least, that was my perception of what was happening. It weighed heavily on me and it scared me. I was always totally exhausted after her visits, partly because I over-compensated for not being with her most of the year. I expect it was to do with a measure of misplaced guilt, which caused me to dance attention on her whilst she stayed with us. I also genuinely wanted to express my love for her in any way I could. So I would make her endless cups of tea and try to make her day as sunny as possible. I think I just wanted to fix it for her and make everything all right again; put it all back together in some way, so she was no longer grieving and living in the past. It never quite worked of course and most evenings I would end up breathing a sigh of relief when she went to bed and then feeling tense, frustrated, resentful and worn out. Linked with this, was the fear that at any time her paranoia would rear its ugly head again and paranoia is very ugly. It twists the mind and poisons relationships. Although I had tried to forget, deep within my sub-conscious lay the impact of damaged relationships, the result of being fed lies which had begun to warp my thinking many years previously. Paranoia is not only ugly it is also extremely destructive, not just for the one consumed by it, but for those on the receiving end of the lies as well. All these years later, there was absolutely no way that I was going to entertain the possibility of my mother polluting my mind with a distortion of truth about my family and friends in Ireland. I was fiercely protective of them and of my own position and rationale. Even so, there had been incidents whilst she had been staying with us, one extremely difficult situation, soon after Rob was born which had involved Trevor. It had resulted in an aftermath of misunderstanding and tension which took its toll on all of us. I certainly would not want to cope with a repeat of that scenario, or any other for that matter.

As I brooded on the situation that day, I began to think about my sister again. A depressive illness had caused her death. It had destroyed her. A depressive illness had also destroyed my mother; at least the mother I remember from my childhood days. Physically, she had not died, but she was no longer the same person. In a way, I felt that I lost her every time she suffered a major breakdown and I most certainly repeatedly grieved for her. I had been assured by the professionals that there was no genetic connection between Mary's illness and my mother's and I believe that to be true. Mary and Jonathan were very close and he was always extremely supportive of her; but I do recall that Mary was going through a particularly stressful time prior to Ian being born. Her father-in law had recently died, she had moved house and most significantly, she had lost a baby daughter. I understand that she heard her baby cry, even though she was born several weeks prematurely. There needed to be a death certificate and the baby officially had to be named. Mary called her little girl Catherine. I remember being with her the day she registered the death and driving her to the coroner's office. To my knowledge, no grief counselling was available in those days. Soon after that, Ian was conceived. I am not an expert and I do not know how much circumstances play a part if any, I just remember that she was dealing with a lot of issues at the time, as well as supporting me in looking after our mother.

Now here I was many years later, still trying to care for my mother and yet thinking I was not succeeding very well. Sitting in the lounge that day mulling over things, I could feel myself losing my grip. Somehow I had to find a way forward and gain control. It had not occurred to me to pray. However, I gradually became conscious of God's presence in the room. It was not in a manner which immediately brought comfort; far from it. The best way is for me to describe it to you visually.

I sensed that God was lifting a curtain in front of me, which had been protecting me from seeing the full extent of how damaging and destructive a paranoid psychosis can be. In my experience, the illness can be all consuming and it manifests itself through an attempt to manipulate and control. God lifted the curtain just a little; enough for me to see the ugliness and the devastation which the condition could reap. It was only for a second, but it was all that was needed for me to confront the darkness of the situation, go through the pain barrier and stare the beast in the eye. It is true to say that the experience traumatised me. But it is also true to say that this same experience was the one which by God's grace, ultimately gave me complete liberty to move forward, without fear of being manipulated or controlled in any way. Once I had looked the beast in the eye, he no longer had a hold over me.

I am not sure how to explain the mechanics behind my change in thinking, but something happened that day in the lounge when God visited me and revealed truth to me. It was a hugely significant turning point in my life as somehow I realised that if I did not take charge, I would constantly fall prey to a manipulative and controlling situation.

My mother came to stay that Christmas as usual, but my relationship with her was very different. It was on a different footing. I was free of any misplaced guilt and I no longer felt that I needed to appease her, seek her approval, or over compensate for not being around for her most of the year. The amazing thing was, I actually felt able to love her in a way that was so much deeper and healthier and releasing for both of us. I did not feel fearful. I did not feel tense. I did not feel exhausted. I held the reins of our relationship with a new found confidence and I enjoyed her company. We drew close in a way which we had not experienced for years and I believe that it was a healing time for both of us. However, for me right then, it was just incredibly freeing.

Christmas is always a busy season for any family and there was as much bustling activity and excitement in our home as in any other. But I managed to juggle my commitments to the boys and all the coming and going, far better than I had done before. When my mother returned to Bristol in the New Year, I hugged her tightly, thanked her for coming, shared with her how much I had valued her time with us and told her that I would be looking forward to her next visit…and I meant it.

18

SOME KIND OF CLOSURE

"Precious in the sight of the Lord is the death of His saints."
Psalm 116.15

The knock on the caravan door wakened me early that morning. Trevor had already left for work as he was commuting each day from Ballywalter to Belfast, which was quite a journey. It was the Easter holidays and as usual, we were staying in our caravan with the boys. Some years previously, we had invested in a static caravan at Sandy Cove, on the Ards Peninsula. The site was small, private and extremely close to the beach. After Capernwray Hall, it was our favourite place. I have many fond memories of great family holidays there, where the relaxation and quietness were such a blessing.

It was the site manager Dennis who needed to speak with me and because it was so early I guessed something was wrong. He explained that Trevor had been in touch with him and that I was to phone back right away, which confirmed my suspicions that all was not well. On hearing Trevor's voice I tried to take in what he was saying, as he broke the news gently to me,

"Viv, your mother has died. Could you pack up, drive home with the boys and I'll meet you there as soon as possible."

It was exactly four months since my mother's Christmas visit to our home and since then, it had proved to be an eventful period of time. At one stage she had been hospitalised, not because of another breakdown, but because of a minor stroke. We had travelled to Bristol to visit her during the boys' half-term break and meetings had been set up with social services to discuss her future. Physically, she had become much more frail and unable to cope on her own and yet like many elderly people, she was unwilling to receive a package of care, fearing so much for her loss of independence. It was a very real dilemma for her and for all the family. Tragically, as we know, this has become an increasingly familiar plight for numerous families in today's society.

I well remember that last visit to Bristol before her death and I have an abiding memory of my mother curled up on her hospital bed in the foetal position, fragile and vulnerable. White hospital stockings covered her legs to help her circulation. Her body was certainly becoming weaker, but her spirit was strong. In time, she recovered well enough to return home and with the support of family and friends she managed to regain most of her independence. A measure of nursing care was set in place, which inevitably she found difficult to accept. A few days before she died, I had phoned her. She was distressed. She was in some pain and she had been advised to go into hospital for tests. Her doctor thought she might have angina. Normally there would have been a resistance to hospitals, but not this time; she seemed to accept it. I reassured her of my love for her, told her that I would return to Bristol as soon as I could and that I was praying for her.

"I know you are my dear." She replied. Unknown to me that was to be the last occasion we would communicate, but our words were tender and consequently very healing. During her final few months, there were times when I had to be firm with her, as had the rest of the family, in order to arrange some sort of support network. As a result, there had inevitably been tension and frustration on both sides. But my final conversation with her had been so sweet and the bond of love between us was tangible. I am very thankful to God for that. Three days after being admitted to hospital, she suffered a massive heart attack. The medical team did everything they could, but they were unable to save her.

However, something marvellous had apparently happened during those three days. On our arrival in Bristol for the funeral, her brothers and sister described to me how they had each noticed a change in her countenance when they had visited her in hospital. They felt that they were with the sister they had known before she was ill. It was as if she had been given back to them. All traces of her mental illness had left her. The oppression, the heaviness of heart, had lifted. Although she was physically weak, her eyes were clearer; her smile was brighter, her thinking more rational. She was able to relax with her siblings, enjoy their company, draw close to them and laugh with them in a way that was reminiscent of their childhood. There was a freedom in her spirit which had been missing for years. Isn't that amazing? It was certainly a source of great comfort for them and also for me. It did not matter that I was not there to witness what had happened; it was enough just to know and to be reassured by the wonder of it. Who could have foreseen that she had only a short time left with us? But for her immediate family, her passing was eased by the miracle of those last few days.

I needed to go to the hospital; I needed to visit the ward where she had died, the bed where it had happened. I needed to speak with the doctors involved and with the nurses. Somehow I was aware that it was necessary to make the events surrounding her death as real as possible. As part of that process, I went with Trevor and our eldest son Rob to the chapel of rest to see my mother for the last time. Death is not so terrible if you know where you are going. A friend of mine, who had just lost a loved one after a long battle with cancer, said that she felt she had accompanied him to the very gates of heaven. That is a very powerful and uplifting statement. However, no one would underestimate that the parting and overwhelming sense of loss can be devastating. Of course I reacted when I saw my mother, but I was also extremely conscious that she was now totally at peace. I had grieved so much for her during her troubled life, how could I not draw comfort from the fact that for her, at last there would be no more pain and no more sorrow? The well known words of Jesus in John ch. 14.1-4 were particularly reassuring.

"Do not let your heart be troubled. Trust in God; trust also in me. In my Father's house are many rooms; if it were not so, I would have told you. I am going there to prepare a place for you; if I go and prepare a place for you, I will come back and take you to be with me that you also may be where I am. You know the way to the place where I am going."

My mother was most certainly a Christian. Because of her illness, she lacked assurance of her faith and she lacked joy. But nothing could rob her of her inheritance in Christ and I knew without a doubt, that she was safe. Some years previously, Trevor and I had been present at her baptism. She had been welcomed and loved by the members of a small Baptist Church in Bristol and it was there that she testified to her faith in Jesus, before she was baptised.

We chose the hymns and the readings for her funeral very carefully. The pastor was most helpful and it was a beautiful service. Many family and friends came back to her home afterwards and I found the time spent with them particularly important. Trevor's brother Alvin had offered to come with us to Bristol and his support and encouragement proved to be invaluable.

Pain is a great leveller and I felt that our shared loss brought me so much closer to my Bristol relatives especially. They were so reassuring and kind. They had lost a sister and I had lost a mother, but the heart doesn't know the difference, only the mind and our grief helped us to form a very deep bond, which exists to this day. It healed any differences and cancelled out any concerns which perhaps had still been there, due to misunderstandings over the years.

I have already mentioned that for a long time I had nursed a fear about the nature of my mother's death. She lived alone in a small flat. She could die alone and no one would know. She might not be found for days. She might take her own life…..she had certainly tried on a few occasions… What if she were to slip in the bath? Her sister was her most frequent visitor. How would she cope if she were to find her unconscious, or worse? How would any of us cope with another suicide in the family? I could not afford to give my imagination free rein, but the thoughts were there, lurking under the surface and sometimes it was hard to keep the lid on them. It can be so very difficult to keep the balance between the harsh reality of a situation and the hope we have, that all will be well.

God understands His children so much better than we understand ourselves. Thank goodness He does. In retrospect, I am aware that He had been preparing me for the time that He would take my mother. I had wasted so much energy worrying about her death, when all He was asking of me was to trust Him. Her last visit to our home had been a huge step forward for me as I have explained and I am so very thankful that God set me free, showing me how to take control of my relationship with her before she died. He had been working up stream on my behalf, paving the way forward. He knew how essential it was for the relationship to be restored and for it to be on a healthy footing; it was linked with moving forward to a place of total healing and wholeness for both of us. It was part of His renewing work in her as well as in me. *Her freedom was at stake too* and I had been doing her no favours, feeding her need to manipulate by appeasing her. In releasing her from my desire for approval, I was unwittingly placing her in God's hands and allowing Him full control of her life…and as it happened, of her death.

She did not slip in the bath. She did not take her own life. She did not die alone in her home. When the heart attack occurred, she was in hospital, surrounded by the best medical help available. Yet her life could not be saved. Why do I gain comfort from that? Because I believe that in God's infinite wisdom and compassion, this was His perfect timing for her and I can rest assured in His words spoken by the prophet Isaiah….

"As the heavens are higher than the earth, so are my ways higher than your ways and my thoughts than your thoughts."
Isaiah 55.9

19

A CHANGE OF SCENERY

"I will instruct you and teach you in the way you should go; I will counsel you and watch over you." Psalm 32.8.

On a clear day, it is possible to see the Mountains of Mourne from Port Erin beach. The Irish Sea stretches some fifty miles westwards from the Isle of Man coast, before its waters lap against Irish soil. Most of the time, the mountains are hidden by clouds and sea mists, but on a day when they are visible, my heart is warmed. I have such a strong affection for Ireland. It was my home for twenty two years. I love the country, the people and Trevor's family, who have become very much my family too. However, in the summer of 1996, just over a year after my mother's death, we left Ireland and set up home on the Isle of Man. It was a huge wrench, but it was right.

The first time we had visited the island, Rob was a toddler and Andrew was a small baby. David and Richard had yet to be born. Trevor had been sent over by the Northern Bank in

Belfast, to implement a computer system for a subsidiary company on the Isle of Man. He estimated that the work would take approximately two months and therefore decided to take his family with him. The boys were too young to be at school, so there was no problem with their education. We stayed in a holiday cottage just outside Douglas, arriving in January when it was particularly cold. I had never set foot on the island before, so it was completely new territory. However, we felt very much at home, although we knew hardly anyone.

Whilst Trevor was at work, the boys and I explored the island and found it to be extremely beautiful. The scenery is not unlike Northern Ireland, but much more accessible, simply because it's on a smaller scale. Parts of the coastline remind me of the Antrim coast road and the mountainous regions inland are as breathtaking as the Mournes. The Glens have their own appeal, especially for walkers and of course the horse drawn trams, the steam trains and the electric railway draw huge crowds, although they only operate during the tourist season.

We both appreciated the way of life on the island. The culture seemed to be more traditional, a little behind with the times in a good way; more laid back. The sense of community was very strong and we were aware that people looked out for one another. Of course that is true in Ireland too, where the family unit is exceptionally strong. However, at the time of our first visit, there was still very much a cloud over Ulster in connection with the "Troubles" and although not directly affected, we certainly felt that lift a little, whilst we stayed on the Isle of Man. Trevor greatly enjoyed his assignment and he was conscious of a professional integrity and a work ethic amongst his colleagues which impressed him.

At some stage during those initial two months on the island, the seed was sown in his mind regarding the possibility of a permanent move to the Isle of Man. However, he was well aware that it would be many years before there would be any likelihood that it could happen and rightly so. Northern Ireland was our home. Our roots were there. Trevor's career was based in Belfast; his wider family circle lived in and around the city. We were settled in the seaside town of Bangor, County Down. The boys had been registered at the local primary school, which had a particularly good name. Education in the area was of an exceptionally high standard. We were hoping that we would be blessed with more children and like all parents, we wanted to be able to provide the best schooling for them. Our lives were busy and full.

So the seed lay dormant for many years…sixteen years in fact. By then, Rob was about to go to Queen's University, Belfast and our other three sons were each at a cut off point in their education. Trevor had taken early retirement and if we were to move at all, this seemed to be the best possible time. To be fair to him, if I had been unhappy about it, he would have honoured my misgivings and I don't think we would have moved. I did have reservations; mainly because of uprooting the children in their teenage years and the effect that would have on them. However, I also saw it as something of an adventure and a whole new start for us, especially after some of the difficulties we had faced in recent years.

We had visited the island several times the year before we made the permanent move, frequently flying with a friend of Trevor's who part owned a small private aeroplane….very scary but much cheaper than commercial flights. We looked at schools and property. In regard to the latter we finally settled on a beautiful house in Port Erin which appeared to meet all our needs. The boys were registered for the new academic year at the nearby comprehensive school in Castletown, where we were impressed with the Headmaster, the atmosphere in the school and the standards achieved.

I don't think we realised at the time, how hard the move was for our sons. They certainly did not share their parents' enthusiasm for a new lifestyle and a new country. They had to take the decision on trust, but it was very difficult for them, especially for Andrew who was then sixteen years old. We had their best interests at heart and they knew that, but in uprooting them from all that was familiar, they suffered a huge loss of identity in almost every area of their young lives. Of course even when change is absolutely right, it can still be very unsettling and it was a particularly long time before Andrew readjusted.

All mothers want to be able to fix it for their children. When they bleed, we bleed. We want to make things better for them, whether that means bathing sore knees when they are little and wiping away tears, or affirming and encouraging them in times of teenage struggles and doubts. However, the Isle of Man move was a completely different ball game. Here was a scenario where as parents, Trevor and I were the very ones who had caused the boys to feel so unsettled and insecure in unfamiliar and alien surroundings. I could not put it right for them and they knew that. In retrospect, I can see perhaps more clearly that the risk we took was enormous. Thankfully, we are a close knit family. Our sons supported one another, pulled together, made friends and at their own pace, each one made a new life for himself here on the island. Today, they are all in their twenties and still based here, well established and pursuing their own careers. However, they will always be Ulstermen. They are proud of their roots and they return to Northern Ireland periodically to visit family and friends. I think they are stronger now and aware that they can cope with change. On a scale of one to ten, the stress of moving to a completely new location is not at the very top of the list, although it is recognised. Families connected with the Armed Forces do it all the time. They have no choice; it goes with the territory and I guess for most of them, it can be an occupational hazard. We did have a choice, but it was not made lightly.

Certainly Trevor has always believed that God directed us to the Isle of Man and why should I seriously doubt that? Ten years further on, it would be true to say that we have no major regrets, although in many ways it has been a steep learning curve. On difficult days, I did wonder if we had made the right decision and whether life would have been easier if we had stayed in Ireland. But it's not about an easy life is it? It's about believing before God that a right decision has been made regardless and being committed to that decision. The grass is always greener and who knows what we might or might not have faced if we had stayed? Since moving, there have been problems and disappointments of course, but also times of great joy and blessing. Trevor returned to banking and later on, took up a position with Coutt's Bank. He very much enjoyed being back in the business world, loved his job and continued working at Coutt's until he was sixty.

Guidance is a strange phenomenon isn't it? As I have grown older, I have come to see that it has less to do with where we happen to live, our circumstances, or our work and much more to do with our relationship with God and maintaining that relationship at all costs. We can become preoccupied with knowing His will when what is far more important is knowing Him. It has been said before that God does not call us to a place first and foremost, but to Himself. I once heard a Bible teacher speak on King David's prayer request from Psalm 51. 12b. *"....and grant me a willing spirit to sustain me."* The speaker explained that God can cope with our mistakes and our failures, so long as our hearts are willing to obey Him, our longing is to know Him and our desire is to love Him. In "My Utmost for His Highest," Oswald Chambers states that the disciple who abides in Jesus *is* the will of God and I guess that sums it up. In that sense, living in Ireland, the Isle of Man or anywhere else is immaterial. Our situation is simply the framework in which God can work out His purposes and transform us into the image of His Son, if we are willing to yield and allow Him to change us. That is my constant challenge and probably yours too.

20

THE STAUROS FOUNDATION

*"Praise be to the God and Father of our Lord Jesus Christ,
the Father of compassion and the God of all comfort, who
comforts us in all our troubles, so that we can comfort those in
any trouble with the comfort we ourselves have received from
God." (2 Corinths.1.3-4)*

When we left Ireland in 1996, there was inevitably a period of
readjustment and settling in to our new lifestyle. With three sons
living at home, I was still very much a housewife and mother,
with plenty to keep me busy on the home front. The church
fellowship we eventually joined was Broadway Baptist, which
is in Douglas. Over the years we have made many close friends
there and we have been involved in various aspects of the life of
the church. But the work which I eventually embraced unfolded
very gradually and was connected with a Welshman called Dewi
Lloyd-Humphreys. Dewi was the full time local representative
for the Stauros Foundation, which is a Christian ministry to

alcoholics and their families. He joined the work in 1992, running a drop-in centre on the Isle of Man and visiting many folks in the community.

The Stauros Foundation was established in Northern Ireland by Arthur Williams. Arthur is an extremely charismatic character, with endless energy and great vision. He is a tough Ulsterman with a tender heart and a wonderful sense of humour. God has gifted him with much wisdom, discernment and compassion. He has pioneered the work since 1971 and the revelation God gave him then, has been the basis of a work which has reached addicts throughout the world with the Gospel of Christ. Both Arthur and Dewi had been alcoholics; both have amazing stories about the way God has set them free from their addiction to drink and both are committed Christians. Because of their backgrounds, they each understand the soul of the alcoholic and they identify totally with his or her plight. The headquarters of the Stauros Foundation is in Co. Armagh, Northern Ireland, where residential care is available, but as the ministry has grown, a branch was opened on the Isle of Man. As well as Northern Ireland, The Stauros Foundation operates in Scotland, the North of England, Southern Ireland (where there is also a residential centre), South America and the U.S.A. I can do no better than to quote from the information booklet on the agency.

"Stauros is the Greek word in the New Testament for the cross of Christ. The Foundation ministers to those who are addicted to alcohol and other drugs and offers support to their families. When the word alcoholic is mentioned, so many people conjure up an image of a "down and out" with no home base. But the majority of alcoholics lie hidden in the structure of society. Of course there are those who require social and material help and there are those who require detoxification and rehabilitation at special centres. Yet many can be reached

before falling to this level. The purpose of the Stauros Foundation is to offer help at whatever point is appropriate. Representatives from the agency, together with many volunteers from the U.K. and beyond, are ministering support and reconciliation to those needy people and their families. The Foundation is an evangelical agency with a Biblical base: believing that all the need prevalent in our society can be met in an experience of conversion to Jesus Christ. In 2. Corinthians 5.17, Paul says, "If any man be in Christ he is a new creature, old things have passed away, behold all things have become new." In embryo, our message is that new life in Christ leads to contented sober living. The Stauros Foundation does not have a set programme for alcoholics or drug addicts to follow. Instead, we endeavour to adopt the general principles of pastoral care that Jesus used in dealing with people. He never ministered in a predetermined way, but rather took each one as an individual. This is not to say that He did not have a clear goal, or that He had no direction in His conversations. He seemed to adopt fundamental principles which allowed Him flexibility in dealing with various situations. Jesus didn't have a programme, but He did have an approach, a way with people. It is our belief that any Christian can, with God's help, reach out effectively to people who have addictions, because it is God who alone can change a person's heart, bring healing to past hurts, forgiveness for past sins and power to live as He intended."

Trevor became involved in the work of Stauros before I did. Every Thursday evening, Dewi led a meeting at the drop-in centre, which was attended by both men and women with addiction problems. There would be a time of worship and an opportunity for sharing, followed by prayer and an encouraging word from Scripture. Hot drinks and sandwiches rounded off the evening. Sometimes Dewi invited a guest speaker to the meeting and that is how Trevor became involved. One Thursday evening, when he was supposed to be speaking, Trevor had to cancel because he was ill. So Dewi asked me instead! He was very persuasive and although a comparatively inexperienced speaker, I agreed. It was with much fear and trepidation that I stepped out from my comfort zone that evening and spoke from the heart on pain and suffering and of the power of God to bring healing and wholeness. Dewi is one of the most Godly men I have ever met. He has no guile, which I think is quite rare and yet he is not naïve. That night, I witnessed him leading the meeting with an amazing combination of compassion, sensitivity and authority. There was such an anointing on his ministry that just in witnessing it, I was greatly blessed. I came away that night, enriched and uplifted by the power of the Holy Spirit and aware that I had touched the reality of God. Although a raw recruit, I was also conscious of a passion in me to reach out to the hurting women within the group, in a way which I had not experienced since being involved in the work of "Rebuilders" in Northern Ireland. There was certainly nothing in me which would naturally be drawn to an alcoholic. But this feeling was not natural. It was far stronger than anything I was capable of experiencing on my own. God had touched my spirit with His Spirit and had kindled a desire in me to express something of His love and acceptance to women who saw themselves as unlovable and unacceptable.

Of course, the presenting problem of alcohol abuse is generally not the core issue. We are focusing here on broken people who are bleeding inside for all sorts of reasons. At some stage they have tried to dull the pain of life and escape by turning to alcohol, only to discover they have become trapped by an even greater spiral of despair and hopelessness.

Needless to say, it was difficult for Dewi to visit the increasing number of women who needed help and as I became more involved, he suggested that I could take on the women's ministry on a voluntary, part time basis. It was of course much more appropriate for me to visit women in their homes than for a man to do so, but I was very aware that I lacked the skills and experience which Dewi possessed. I had been learning on the job and that had been invaluable, as had my debriefing sessions with Dewi. I have always felt very comfortable in his company, partly because he is so affirming and totally non-judgemental. Arthur Williams was also extremely encouraging. He comes over from Northern Ireland on a regular basis to monitor the work and to offer support and guidance for the local team. It was certainly very important to me, having that level of accountability. In time, we opened a ladies' drop-in on Friday mornings and although our numbers were small, God was constantly encouraging and equipping us. As with any support group, the key to moving forward was unconditional trust and acceptance. Although there were disappointments, a small nucleus of women met each week. They were committed to one another and to the common goal of being totally free from the hold which drink had over them. As they shared their stories, I was aware that I needed to remember the well worn statement, "There but by the grace of God go I." We are all vulnerable and who's to say that I would not have ended up an alcoholic if I had been sexually abused as a child, or abused in some other way? Dr. John Townsend, the eminent Christian Psychiatrist, wrote a book called "Hiding from Love" in which he makes this highly significant statement.

"As children, our hiding patterns may have protected us from a threatening environment. But what serves as protection for a child, can become a prison to an adult, isolating us from the very things we need to heal and mature."

In order for me to gain more experience and understanding as to how to help the women, Arthur arranged for me to go to Glasgow and stay with Linda Mc.Credie. Linda is the Stauros representative and full time worker with women in Scotland, having joined the team in 1999. She is a qualified teacher and social worker, who had been drawn into the world of alcohol and drug abuse at an earlier stage in her life. However, she now testifies to God's grace and healing power in delivering her from the hold addiction had over her. Linda welcomed me into her home and I stayed with her for about five days, shadowing her as she worked with, counselled and supported many needy women.

Certainly I benefited from the training whilst I was with her, but she had such professional expertise and compassion, linked with years of experience that I felt I was still on the starting blocks. However, that did not matter; it was not really the issue. What spoke to me most and challenged me more than anything else, was her zeal, her enthusiasm and her commitment to her "girls" as she called them. She believed that no one was beyond hope and she worked tirelessly to that end. Her passion and her drive were inspirational; her ministry exceptional. Like Dewi, she could be extremely tender and understanding if that was appropriate, but she could also be tough if necessary. Everything she did was seasoned with warmth and humour, as she constantly sought to speak truth into her girls' lives. They adored her.

Sadly, I think it is quite rare to meet people who are one hundred per cent aware that they have found their God-given calling. Many of us are still square pegs in round holes. Being in the centre of God's will is the most liberating and the most fulfilling place to be. It is the place where we are most secure, most real and most energised, because all God's resources are available to us. It is the place where we find our true identity and where we are most likely to reflect the beauty of Jesus. It is the place where we soar. John Piper put it very clearly when he made this powerful observation, *"God is most glorified in us, when we are most satisfied in Him."*

In meeting Linda, I discovered that kind of reality is not only possible, but it can be sustained, despite inevitable setbacks and heartaches. The key is commitment to the call of God and a willing spirit to persist against all odds. Knowing God and knowing His calling merge into one. Out of that, is born a joy and a freedom which is not only irrepressible, but also infectious. It certainly gives much more meaning to Nehemiah's encouraging words, *"Do not grieve, for the joy of the Lord is your strength."* (Neh.8.10b.) Note where Nehemiah was when he made that statement. Significantly, even though he faced opposition, he knew without a doubt, that he was right in the centre of God's will.

I must have worked as a volunteer with the Stauros Foundation for about six years. Amongst the friendships I made during that time, there were three women to whom I drew especially close. As I write, one of the three has not touched a drink for seven months. The second has not drunk for almost four years. Both are professional middle-class women and both would have at one stage, drunk several bottles of vodka a week. It is a testimony to the grace of God and to their own determination that they are on their way to a life of sobriety. The third, Tracy, (I use her name with her permission) has in the last two years, taken over my role and is doing the most amazing work.

God liberated Tracy from alcohol addiction about three years ago. It happened in quite a dramatic way, although of course there is no blue-print to the way in which God works. She would say that although God delivered her and she no longer has a craving for drink, she still has a choice to make each day as to whether she goes down that road again. She takes responsibility for the decisions she makes and I think that's important to remember. God does not take away our free will. But the beauty of her being involved in the work is that like Arthur, Dewi and also Linda, Tracy identifies with the heart of the problem. She can truly say to the addicts that she understands the cycle of despair in which they are ensnared. However, she can and also does speak of the God who loves us unconditionally and who offers hope, healing and forgiveness for those who are prepared to reach out in faith; even if their faith is as small as a mustard seed. That's all that Jesus says we need, whatever our situation. In reality, I'm not sure we very often have much more than that. Eph.3.20, 21 are verses to which I have already referred. The apostle Paul reminds us here of the divine nature of God, stating in his eulogy that,

"He is able to do immeasurably more than all we ask or imagine, according to His power that is at work within us, to Him be glory in the Church and in Christ Jesus throughout all generations for ever and ever."

Isn't it good therefore, that God understands His children. We can be sure that as long as our mustard-seed faith is rooted in Him, He responds to our cry in a way that releases His power within us, for our underlying well-being, but also ultimately for His glory.

21

THOSE YOU HAVE GIVEN ME

"The one who calls you is faithful and He will do it."
(1 Thess.5.24)

"God doesn't expect you to fix it for everyone Viv." The kind words of a friend were said to reassure and encourage me. Of course they were words which I already knew to be true, but I still needed to be reminded of them. I was becoming more and more involved with the ladies I had met through working with the Stauros Foundation and finding it increasingly difficult to balance that work with family and other commitments. I was extremely tired. No one was putting pressure on me; I was doing that for myself.

Most women are mother hens I believe, regardless of whether or not they have children. I am no exception. I want to rescue people and straighten out their lives. It sounds commendable doesn't it, but in reality, the "feel good" factor can take over and dominate my thinking. Quite often it seems to me, that what I do for others is tarnished to some extent by self interest. Our motives are rarely pure and in helping other people we can end up massaging our own egos with generous doses of philanthropic oils. I suspect that you will agree with me and I just want to be honest. The need is not the call and I am only too aware that I am much too eager to dive in to any situation, without sufficient fore-thought as to whether I am the most appropriate person to help, or whether in fact, my sympathy is misplaced.

I am learning the hard way; partly because as I grow older, tiredness takes over more quickly and I just do not have the same energy levels. I am learning to say "No" and I am learning that I can do so without feeling guilty and that in any case, God probably doesn't want me to get in His way. No one is indispensable. Having said that, we all need to be needed and we all need to be valued. Reaching out in compassion can have the two fold purpose of genuinely helping another, as well as fulfilling a need in us to have some kind of validity in the Christian arena. We can so easily fall into the trap of looking for brownie points. I know my own heart and the mixed motives which sometimes compete for attention. I don't think a kind deed is necessarily negated. It just shows that we all have feet of clay and that we want people to think well of us. However, the question of motive is extremely important, so whom are we trying to impress? Our goal is always to become more Christ-like and His motives were consistently one hundred per cent pure.

Jesus never ran Himself ragged chasing after every needy person. He did not allow Himself to be manipulated. He was always in control of His relationships and His integrity was not threatened or compromised. When He did reach out to people it was never to feed a need in Himself first and foremost, although ministering to others certainly brought Him great joy. It was not about seeking to impress, or about His own reputation. He laid that on the line continually. In fact, Scripture reminds us that *"He made Himself of no reputation..."* (Phil.2.7a. King James). So how did He prevent Himself from being pulled in all directions?

As Jesus prays to His Father, we read these words in John 17.4, *"I have brought you glory on earth by completing the work you gave me to do."* How could He be certain that He had finished the work God had given Him, when there was still so much need? Jesus did not waste time or energy on any other business but His Father's. What was on God's heart became His sole agenda...

"The man up the tree Father? Right, I'm on my way. The one over there Father, by the Pool of Bethesda? Leave it to me. That lonely Samaritan woman, drawing water from the well? Yes, of course I'll help her."

We could say that Jesus had a unique hot-line to heaven, but that would be a cop out, because the real key to His relationship with His Father was intimacy. He was in such close contact, that He knew His Father's voice and it gave Him a deep sense of fulfilment to respond in obedience. Jesus endorses this in John 8.29, when He states, *"The one who sent me is with me; He has not left me alone, for I always do what pleases Him."*

It is this same closeness with God which He longs for us to have and it is this intimacy which embraces much of His prayer to His Father in John 17. If I had to choose an over-all favourite passage from the Bible, it would be this chapter. I love it because it is a window into the heart of Jesus. We are listening in to His deepest desires for God's children, born out of His own intimacy with His Father. Not only does Jesus long for us to have the same unity with the Father that He enjoys, but also, out of that intimate relationship, He wants believers to have a oneness which will reflect His Father's love. Jesus is still interceding in the same way today. His prayer is timeless. I find that both comforting and challenging.

"I have given them the glory that you gave me that they may be one as we are one: I in them and you in me. May they be brought to complete unity to let the world know that you sent me and have loved them even as you have loved me." (John 17.22, 23)

Jesus prays with a passion, that we might know the Father as He does…intimately. If we are close to someone, we would certainly recognise his voice when he is speaking. Do we know the Father's voice? Do we spend enough time in His presence to become familiar with His voice? Do we know whom He wants us to encourage and support? There is so much need; it is vital that we learn to recognise the voice of our Father and respond as Jesus did. If we don't, we will end up spreading ourselves too thinly, carrying burdens that God never intended us to carry. We will be operating under our own steam and feeling exhausted and frustrated at the end of each day. What use are we to anyone then?

I think it is extremely significant in John 17, when Jesus states that He is not praying for the world, but for *"those whom God has given Him."* He makes this statement on at least three occasions in the same chapter. Is this the key? Over and above my family, I need to know exactly whom God is giving me, so that by faith, I can intercede for them, minister to them and help in what ever way He leads me to do so. This is the constant challenge and I can only fulfil it as I learn to discern His voice and nurture the discipline of listening when He is speaking to me. Amongst all the other voices which clamour for my attention, I need to recognise the still small voice of my Father; the voice with which Jesus was so familiar.

Referring to Himself as the Shepherd, in John 10.4, Jesus states, *"When He has brought out all His own, He goes on ahead of them and His sheep follow Him because they know His voice.*" Perhaps I need to learn a lesson from sheep. They may have a reputation for being stupid, but at least they know their Master's voice and have the wisdom to follow Him in simple trust and obedience. I believe that's all God really requires of us.

Now I have to ask myself the question, "How much do I really want to hear the voice of my Father?" I love to hear His voice if He is going to comfort me, or encourage me. But what if He is calling me to do something or go somewhere I don't want to go, or visit someone I don't want to visit? God's voice demands a response from me and it could be costly. There is a risk involved. The Children of Israel were aware of this when they said to Moses, *"...Speak with us yourself and we will listen. But do not have God speak to us, or we will die."* (Ex.20.19)

They knew they would have to do something about it, if God spoke to them. They could not afford to ignore it. But if it was just a messenger addressing them, they could explain it away. (Oswald Chambers points this out in "My Utmost for His Highest." Feb. 12th.) I have known times when I have heard the voice of God in my life, but I have chosen to ignore it, or explain it away, because to respond appeared to be too costly. I have also known times when I have resisted God's voice and had no peace until I have finally given in and said "Yes" to Him. Then the awareness of His presence and the sense of freedom which follows can be quite overwhelming. There is a quickening in my spirit; apprehension gives way to anticipation and excitement, as the life of Christ is released in me and rises up to meet the challenge.

Watchman Nee once made this statement, *"We can't expect the Lord to live out His life in us, if we don't give Him our lives in which to live."* Like the Apostle Paul, Watchman Nee had lived his life on the front line of the battlefield. He had been called to endure much adversity for the sake of his faith in

Christ. Few of us in the Western World suffer in the same way, but as believers, we need constantly to take on board the powerful and inspiring words of this amazing Chinese missionary. God knows our strengths and He knows our weaknesses. He identifies how He has gifted us and which of His children is most suited to fulfil a role. He recognises the ways in which we need to push our boundaries, take risks and mature in our faith, even when events appear to be extremely threatening. We can trust Him, just as the terrified disciples learnt to do on the Sea of Galilee, when Jesus calmed the raging storm.

"....For it is God who works in you to will and to act according to His good purpose."(Phil.2.13). Paul made this statement with great conviction, because he had proved God's faithfulness. He was confident that God would always provide the resources needed to accomplish His will, however daunting the task might appear to be. God is in control and He is faithful. He does not call without equipping. It is His work, first and foremost, not mine and to accomplish it, He gives me His covering, His anointing and His authority. However, for my own protection and well-being, He also gives me boundaries and I ignore them at my peril.

One day, as believers, we will receive our reward in heaven and we will each hear the words, *"Well done, good and faithful servant."* So why should I need to give myself brownie points for my feeble, self-imposed charitable efforts, when the King of Kings has invited me to be a co-worker with Him, helping to establish His Kingdom here on earth? If I can keep that in focus and learn to recognise and respond in faith to His voice more often, I might have a chance of completing the work God has given me to do; even if in my misguided enthusiasm to fix it for everyone, I go off in the wrong direction from time to time.

22

RESTORATION

"I am still confident of this: I will see the goodness of the Lord in the land of the living. Wait for the Lord; be strong and take heart and wait for the Lord."(Psalm 27.13, 14)

The official looking brown envelope dropped onto my door mat about mid-day. The post never arrives much before lunch-time in our area on the Isle of Man, because most has to be flown over from the mainland each day. I do not recall whether there were any other letters on that particular morning in February, 2001. If there were, they were of little significance compared with the impact which the contents of the brown envelope were to have on me. I assumed that the letter was from the Dept. of Health, advising me of the results of some recent routine medical tests I had undergone. Initially I just browsed at the contents, with half my attention still on the Radio 4 news programme droning away in the background. It was a while before the heading at the top of the page registered with me.

"Salvation Army Family Tracing Service." But it was the last line of the letter which caused my whole being to react in a way which was totally beyond the realm of normal suburban domestic behaviour.

"Ian is hoping that you are the sister of his late mother." Had I read that correctly?

I turned off the radio.......... *"IAN IS HOPING THAT YOU ARE THE SISTER OF HIS LATE MOTHER."*

My son Richard was in the kitchen, so he was the only one to witness his mother's consequent bizarre behaviour. He told me at a later date that he was quite frightened and had wondered when the men in white coats would arrive to take me away. I cried, I laughed, I shouted for joy. I was unable to verbalise what had happened; no doubt I was in shock. I seem to remember hyper-ventilating, or something similar and I think I danced on a chair at one stage. If there had been any around, I'm sure I would have happily swung from the chandeliers.

Eventually, I regained my equilibrium sufficiently to be able to lift the telephone and try to speak with Trevor who was at a meeting. Unable to reach him, I managed to contact my family in Bristol, Trevor's brother Alvin and close friends. Aware that she would be as thrilled as I was, I also spoke with Gill, Ian's aunt, who was still living in Bristol and who had looked after Paul and Ian so well, immediately after Mary had died. Who else could I telephone with the wonderful news that my sister's son had finally found me after over thirty years? I wanted the whole of the Isle of Man to know and would readily have placed a full page spread in the local newspaper if the editor had been in agreement. Still in a state of euphoria, I re-read the letter from the Salvation Army and realised that there was a contact number where I could gain more information. As a result of my call and in exchange for my own details, I was given Ian's address, telephone number and precious information about him. I spent the next few hours trying to compose the most significant, meaningful letter that I had probably ever written and also tenderly choose a small selection of family photographs to send to him. He was living in the North of England, with his wife and little boy and he was training to be a doctor. That evening, I asked Trevor to telephone him and speak with him first, as I was unsure whether I would cope. I heard him say,

"Ian, this is your Irish uncle." And then Trevor handed me the phone…..

We must have spoken together for about an hour. Neither of us wanted to end the conversation or put the phone down. Neither of us seemed like strangers to each other. The conversation just flowed and it was very natural. I could have been speaking with one of my sons. We realised that we had both sat down that afternoon and written to each other and that our letters would most likely cross in the post. The next day, I pored over Ian's letter; read it and re-read it until I practically knew it by heart. He too, had included photographs of himself, his wife Jane and Timothy, their little boy. Ian looked so much like his mother. He also resembled my son Andrew and Jane looked just lovely. In his letter, Ian explained that he and his brother had never known what had happened to their mother. Whenever they tried to ask their father, he was unable to talk about it. They assumed that perhaps she had died in a car crash. They did not know if their mother had any family and they were certainly totally unaware of my existence. I had discovered from our telephone conversation that after they had lived in Africa for some time, they moved on, but eventually returned to England because their step-mother's daughter Jennie had become seriously ill and needed expert care.

Ian decided on a career change in his late twenties, when he started to train as a doctor. He explained to me that it was while he was having to take details of patients' family histories, coupled with the birth of his first son that he began to wonder about his own roots and especially his mother's family. So with Jane's full backing and support, he subsequently took the decision to probe more deeply and make some tentative enquiries. Not knowing what he might uncover, he was initially able to track down my mother's death certificate. Trevor was the executor of her estate, so his signature was on the certificate. Taking note of his name, Ian then read the words, "Relationship to deceased." To which Trevor had answered, "Son in law." Ian realised at that point that his mother must have had a sister, although he did not know my Christian name. As he continued his search, he kept drawing a blank and so eventually he put the investigation into the hands of the Salvation Army Family Tracing Service. What a marvellous service! I had never heard of that branch of the Salvation Army before, but I am full of praise for the superb work they do and have since heard of wonderful stories of the way in which they have brought families together.

Ian and I had many questions to ask each other and we were both looking forward so very much to a reunion after all these years. We arranged to meet at the Lowry Centre in Manchester, two weeks after the initial telephone call. Trevor and I took the ferry from the Isle of Man on that Saturday and I remember spending ages trying to decide what to wear for the trip. I just wanted to look my very best! I carried with me a large box of family photographs plus Mary's gold watch and a gold necklace she had owned. We had never been to the Lowry Centre before and we had difficulty finding it, but eventually we discovered some brown signposts in the middle of Manchester, pointing us in the right direction. We had planned to meet in the small café attached to the Centre and as we walked towards the building with its glass panelling, I could see that Ian and Jane were already there. They were sitting at a small table drinking coffee, or tea, or something hot; I can't remember what it was and it doesn't matter. It is hard to describe the next few moments. Certainly there were tears; precious, joyful tears as we hugged one another. We were strangers, yet not strangers; not for one moment. My soul reached out to Ian to touch the heart of this young man whom I had longed to embrace over the years. There was a little shyness, but only a little. All of Mary's love for her son appeared to be channelled into that moment of meeting and for a while, it was as if she lived again. The value and reality of family had never taken on a more significant and all embracing meaning as we experienced the amazing opportunity of drawing close to each other. How could we begin to fill the enormous gap in our lives created by the separation of thirty years? Yet in a sense there was no gap; no separation. We were a kindred spirit; we were family and somehow that knowledge transcended any sense of time and lifted us to a plain beyond the years of division.

Ian had only one photograph of his mother. His search had taken him to the home where Mary had died and a neighbour, still living next door, had given the photograph to him. It was of a group, taken at the play-school which his brother Paul had attended as a toddler. Mary is looking downwards, gathering Paul up in her arms. Her face is hidden. Ian had never seen his mother's face. The box of photographs I had brought contained a life time of memories for me. Many of the earlier ones were black and white; photographs of two little girls playing in the sand at Weston-Super-Mare with their parents; holiday snaps taken at the farm in North Devon, which as children, Mary and I had loved so much. We sifted through the contents of the box, Ian studying every photograph while I gently gave my nephew as much information as I could about the family members in each picture. So many questions to answer; so many pieces of the jigsaw to fit together and always at the back of my mind, the deep concern that I might have to answer honestly a question about the exact nature of Mary's death.

Ian seemed to sense my concern and explained to me that he had discovered what had happened. The day his mother died, a young policeman had been posted outside her bedroom door. During his search thirty years later, Ian had visited the coroner's office in Bristol and had spoken with the assistant coroner. It transpired that this same man was the very policeman standing on duty outside the bedroom. He remembered the case. He was able to answer many of his questions, which were very searching. Ian wanted to know everything. It must have been extremely painful for him, piecing every detail together and our meeting on that day at the Lowry Centre was of course, part of that process for both of us. He had already learned most of what had occurred on that fateful day, but I was able to answer a few remaining queries regarding the facts. However, I should have anticipated what Ian really needed to know.

"Tell me about my mother. What was she like?"

And so I began to describe to him the mother he had never known and the sister I had lost. I wanted to do Mary justice, which was not difficult because she was such a lovely person. I described her personality, her likes and dislikes, her friendships and her achievements. She was an excellent nurse, which was acknowledged when she won the gold medal; the highest award bestowed on just one nurse each year at the hospital where she trained. But what I especially wished to focus on was her relationship with Jonathan and her two sons. I wanted Ian to be reassured as to how much his parents loved each other; how happy they were together, which was most certainly reflected in the photographs I gave him. Mary adored her sons, as Jonathan did too; they were excellent parents and with the children they had become a close knit, secure family.

During our conversation, Ian made a comment which brought tears to my eyes, although they were never far from the surface.

"I had hoped my mother had been buried, so that I could have put flowers on her grave, but she was cremated wasn't she?" I was not expecting that question and I was unsure about the best way to respond. I found myself explaining that Ian was right; his mother had been cremated. However, I went on to say that Mary was a believer; she was a Christian, as Trevor and I were. I knew that I would see her again in heaven. That was not a false hope; it was the truth. She could not come to be with me, but one day I could go to be with her. I have always drawn much comfort from that fact, because it is our reality, it is our hope and most importantly, it is God's Word.

Ian and Jane had not brought their son Timothy with them to the Lowry Centre; he was not quite two years old and it would have been a long day for him. They had left him in the care of close friends, but had arranged for us to call in and meet him later that day. And so, whilst drinking a cup of tea in their friends' home, I watched this beautiful little boy playing in the garden with his toys and with other children. I observed him from a distance. I did not want to frighten him or overwhelm him. This was Mary's grandson. How much she would have loved him. He was of course totally unaware of the drama which had been unfolding during the day. I smiled as I watched him, content in knowing that he was such a happy, secure and much loved child, with two wonderful parents. Trevor and I probably stayed longer than we should have and it was a race against time to drive back to Liverpool and catch the returning ferry for the Isle of Man. Before leaving, Timothy and I had begun to draw close, as we had played with his toys together and he had let me hug him. Precious photographs were taken for a keepsake of the most amazing day, which we all knew would be the first of many. I had searched for the right words to say to Ian as we parted. I cannot remember everything I said to this fine young man who had courageously taken the risk of discovering the truth, but I do recall embracing him and making this heart felt statement. "You remind me so much of your mother Ian …and I could not pay you a greater compliment."

I closed my eyes on the journey home and tried to sleep. The ferry was crowded with day-trippers, many returning from Liverpool after successful shopping expeditions and there was a buzz of activity. I was emotionally and physically exhausted, but sleep constantly managed to evade me. My mind was on overdrive. I began to think about my mother. Some years before she died, she had discovered that a law had been passed which gave grandparents legal access to grandchildren. It had filtered through that the children were still abroad with their father and step-mother, but all she had to go on was a P.O. Box number. She took steps to fight for her right to be reunited with her grandchildren. It potentially proved to be an extremely expensive case which she could not afford, so she applied for legal aid. After being refused aid, appealing against that decision and losing, she had no alternative but to drop the case. Apparently the lawyers representing legal aid felt that her grandsons would soon be old enough to make contact with her themselves. She had pointed out that they might not know of her existence, which of course proved to be right. It was a huge travesty of justice that she never saw her grandchildren again and one which causes me deep sadness. She would have crawled over broken glass to be with them and it never happened, which meant that they too were denied the opportunity to know their grandmother and enjoy the benefit of other close family relationships. However, I am also aware that to force the issue, not knowing what the boys had been told about their mother's relatives, could have been counter-productive. What we did *not* know until I met Ian was that he and his brother were actually sent to boarding school in Bristol. My mother could have passed them on the street and been unaware that she had just brushed shoulders with her grandsons.

About two years before I received the letter from the Salvation Army, I had been very tempted to try to find my two nephews myself. Thinking about them came over me in waves, but at that particular time, they were more on my mind than usual. Circumstances had arisen which had caused me to focus on where they might be and I ached for them. I remember speaking with a family friend who, like Trevor, wisely suggested that I should wait and perhaps one day, the boys would want to find me. He reminded me of a verse from the Psalms; in fact it's just part of a verse.

"*Deep calls to the deep......*" (Psalm 42:7a.) I'm sure there is more than one interpretation of that statement and I don't want to take it out of context, but the friend shared with me how this verse may well refer to the deep longing of the soul. He suggested that there might be an ache in my nephews' hearts too and a longing for something which escaped them; something which they could not quite understand. Could they in fact be calling out for me, without realizing it? Maybe they were actually already searching for me. This possibility settled my heart; I was able to shelve my thoughts on the matter, refocus and wait for God's timing. Perhaps you can see why I have shared this with you. It was approximately two years from the day that Ian began his search, to the day when I received the letter from the Salvation Army. Both he and I felt the stirring of the soul about the same time. There was a very real sense in which we had been calling out to each other. Meeting at the

Lowry Centre, meant that the longing was satisfied, at least in part. The jigsaw was not quite complete however, because Paul and I had not yet been reunited and that would take a little more waiting and a little more time.

23

Full Circle

"The Lord will restore the years which the locusts have eaten away…….."   (Joel.2.25a. King James)

The day that Mary died, I have a very clear picture of two year old Paul, sitting on his father's lap asking where his mother was. With tears running down his face, Jonathan embraced his son and explained as simply and as gently as he could, that Mary had died. Paul did not fully understand of course and I remember him wiping the tears from his father's face. Who can tell how much a little child is able to digest of such traumatic events and of how he deals with the magnitude of such a loss? Perhaps that has something to do with the fact that unlike Ian, he was extremely reticent about searching for his mother's family and was initially unwilling to join his brother in his search. Paul remembered nothing of the events of that dreadful day and very little of any significance until the move to Africa about two years later. I do understand that a reunion with his mother's family, could open the lid on suppressed thoughts and emotions and I certainly did not want to pressurise Paul into meeting us before he felt absolutely ready. Ian was only five months old when his mother died, so maybe it was a little easier for him to pursue the truth, although I think he showed tremendous tenacity and guts in his search for his family and in his desire to know exactly what had happened.

It was to be over a year before Paul and I finally met. During that time, Ian, Jane and Timothy came to stay with us on the Isle of Man and we visited them in their home in Yorkshire, both of which were extremely happy occasions. Since our first meeting, Jane had given birth to a second son called Mark who, like his brother, is an absolute delight.

In July, 2002, my eldest son Rob was planning to be married in Barcelona. His fiancée Becky had lived there all her life because her English father has worked in Spain as a pastor and missionary for over thirty years. Becky's mother is American and she is involved in pastoral work along side her husband. As well as his immediate family, Rob was keen to invite all his first cousins to the wedding. So Rob and Becky sent a wedding invitation to Paul, via Ian. Included with the invitation, was a letter I had written, explaining that although we would love Paul, his wife Karen and their two children to come to the wedding, we would totally understand if they felt unable to do so. A wedding is an emotional event at the best of times, so it was probably not the most appropriate occasion to throw in a family reunion as well! As it happened, Paul did not come to the wedding, but about two months before it took place, I received a phone call from Ian to let me know that his brother felt ready to make contact and that he probably would be writing to me quite soon.

After my initial excitement at receiving this news, a strange heaviness settled on me which I could not understand, nor could

I control. I began to feel an overwhelming sense of sadness which was out of all proportion to my circumstances. In fact, there was nothing in my life at that time which warranted emotional distress and yet each day, the intensity of my pain increased. And then the tears began. I would make a cup of tea and the tears would come. I would do the ironing and the tears would begin. I would go shopping and find myself weeping again. During those difficult and confusing weeks, tears became my constant companion and I seemed to have no control over when they would start or when they would cease. As my anguish increased, I became very scared. I did not understand where all this pain was coming from, nor did I know what to do with it. The heartache was becoming all consuming. It was not depression; it was grief, although of course the two are connected. However, I had no way of knowing how to handle what was happening. Mary had died over thirty years ago; but it was yesterday and it was as if her coffin was in the next room. I have never known before or since such intense raw pain. It invaded every part of my being and rendered me helpless to resist the crippling effect on my increasingly fragile psyche. I was becoming unable to function normally or focus on the simplest task, which was very frightening. And all the time, the tears continued to flow.

Emotional pain by its very nature is self-absorbing. It screams at us that it wants to be noticed; it relentlessly demands attention. My pain was leaking from the heart to the soul in a way that was crushing me and suffocating both the desire and ability to fight back. I was sinking in the quicksand of sorrow and grief and there was no rope; no life-line.

In my distress, I contacted Joan, a close friend of mine who was a social worker and also a grief counsellor at the local hospice. She explained that what was happening to me was not unusual and that it had a name. Apparently, I was experiencing "frozen grief." It could occur years after the death of a loved one and was the result of internalising grief; not allowing it to be expressed in a healthy way at the time of the death and consequently burying it as far down as possible in the deepest corner of the heart. Quite literally, I discovered, I had numbed my pain. I thought I had dealt with the loss at the time of Mary's death, but it is true that I was focused on supporting my mother through the trauma and had little time to work through my own grief. I had not intentionally suppressed it, but subconsciously, that was exactly what I had done. The anticipation of Paul contacting me was simply the trigger needed to bring everything to the surface and because it had been buried and pressed down for so long, the pain was far more intense and overwhelming than if I had dealt with it at the right time. Understanding what was happening helped to quell my anxiety, but did not stop the anguish or the tears. Joan explained to me that I must allow my grief to take its course and that in time I would be free from it and with the freedom would come healing. I could see the logic in that and had become aware that it was necessary to allow the grief to surface, although I would have been happy for it to remain dormant, given the anguish it was causing me!

Another close friend of mine gave me very wise counsel during this time. Jean and I were neighbours and we had met together regularly over the years to pray specifically for our children. Knowing how much I was struggling, she drew my attention to Isaiah. 61. 1-3. The passage about the healing ministry of Jesus is a favourite of mine, but on this occasion Jean focused on the last part of verse 3........

"They will be called oaks of righteousness, a planting of the Lord for the display of His splendour."

Yes, we know that Jesus came to heal the broken hearted, but that is not an end in itself. Our healing is a living testimony to the faithfulness of an almighty God, who is in the business of restoring His people. In the process, they must essentially reflect something of His glory and of His splendour. I had never seen that before in the context of these verses, until Jean pointed it out. Now perhaps, I had something I could hold onto…a goal. If the situation in which I found myself was moving me to a place of healing where God would be glorified, maybe I could stay the course and hang in there. At least it gave a foundation for the pain and hopefully could help lift me to a level where I would no longer be floundering in despair and I could try to focus on something beyond myself. Could the reality of this truth be the safety-net which would rescue me from becoming totally self-absorbed? Certainly, I have come to see that Isaiah 61 v 3 describes an extremely important biblical principle and one which I have since explored more fully, but at that time, I was only able to apply it on a good day. To be honest I continued to limp along more or less in the same confused state of mind, for about six weeks. Then, one evening around 10pm, the telephone rang. Richard took the call… "There's a man on the phone wanting to speak with you Mum." I remember being particularly tired that evening and not feeling like speaking with anybody. Dragging myself up from my comfortable chair, I reluctantly took the phone from my son….. "Vivien, this is Paul."…… "Paul who?" I replied rather abruptly……"Your nephew Paul," He answered.

24

A SPECIAL PRIVILEGE

"He tends His flock like a shepherd; He gathers the lambs in His arms and carries them close to His heart; He gently leads those that have young." (Isaiah. 40. V.11)

Standing in the arrivals lounge at Ronaldsway Airport, I began to study the passengers through the glass partition. They were making their way along the corridor to the carousel where luggage was already being collected. It was late summer, 2002, and holiday makers were still arriving on the Isle of Man to enjoy the beaches, the beautiful countryside and hopefully some sunshine. More than one family was waiting by the carousel, but I was almost sure that I would be able to recognise Paul and Karen and their two children from the photographs Paul had sent me. A few weeks had passed since that first phone call from Paul. Almost immediately after he had contacted me, the grief which had engulfed me and had been such an unwelcome tenant, behaving like a squatter, just disappeared. It left as suddenly as it had arrived, but not before it had accomplished its work. It had forced me to take ownership of a much neglected deep-rooted sorrow which had lain dormant in the unplumbed recesses of my heart for far too long, gathering dust and debris along the way. But taking ownership involved confronting the past and then embracing the full force of its impact on me; in short, feeling the rawness of the pain, letting go of it and eventually moving forward.

Significantly, my Bible readings around this time were focused on dealing with grief. (U.C.B. "The Word for Today, May 2002) The writer mentions Matthew 5.v.4, where Jesus states,

"Blessed are those who mourn, for they shall be comforted."
and then goes on to say that it is necessary to embrace the one in order to receive the other. He quotes from "A better Kind of Grieving," by Bill Hybels. *'Fifty years ago, industrialists thought they could just bury toxic waste and it would go away. We've since learnt that it doesn't. It leaks into the water, contaminates the crops and kills the animals. Burying grief does the same thing. It leaks into our emotional system and wreaks havoc. It distorts our perception of life and taints our relationships."* The writer continues by explaining that the process of becoming whole involves (a) feeling deeply (b) dealing honestly (c) making way for healing. He states that sometimes we try to find quick relief by releasing the grief before we have gone through it, because we fear the process. We run from the pain or try to replace it with another feeling as soon as we can, which only makes things worse. He refers to Psalm 30.5b *".......weeping may endure for a night but joy cometh in the morning."* commenting that we must go through one in order to get to the other. I guess that is what God had allowed me to do and I am glad that the process had run its course before

meeting Paul. The part of my heart which needed to be restored had been restored. Certainly, I would far rather walk through this broken bleeding world, hand in hand with my Father than face heartache on my own, resentful of the premise that God had permitted the suffering in the first place and blaming Him for allowing it. The writer of "Word for Today." concludes his thoughts on dealing with grief by describing what happened when Moses died…

"Moses was the greatest leader Israel ever had .His death was an unspeakable loss. Together God's people wept on the Plains of Moab. For thirty days and nights, God stood by, allowing them to mourn in a healthy expression of grief….no hurrying, no divine censure, no denial. Only when God saw that they had completed the process, did He tell Joshua to lead them forward……They had to go through, to get through! We all need to do the same."

So here I was, waiting to embrace my nephew Paul, free from the ghosts of the past and looking forward to meeting his wife and children for the very first time. What a joy and what a very precious time we shared together as we drew closer each day and Paul and I rekindled emotional ties. He is so different from his brother, but a fine young man in every way with a wonderful wife and two great children, Ross and Anna.   There have been several reunions since that first initial visit to the Isle of Man. Ian had already been to Bristol and had been reunited with Gill and Thomas and with the extended family on his mother's side and Paul went on to do the same. Both experiences were extremely moving to witness as the two brothers re-established relationships with their family. It was particularly poignant when they met with Gill and Thomas who had looked after them so well following their mother's death. But for me personally, the most heart-felt experience was being with my two nephews *together* for the very first time when they both visited our home with their families. It was as if the events of the past thirty years or more truly had come full circle, as a tide of emotion surfaced and treasured memories of embracing two little boys so long ago began to flood my mind. It was also very good that Paul had now caught up with Ian and that they were of one mind in finding their roots and reaping the benefit of that decision; which as a family, we were doing as well. Wisely, they are waiting for the right time to share the news with their father, aware of how emotionally fragile he is in this area. Maybe one day I shall be able to embrace him too, but that is outside my control and rightly so.

Now, I would like to explain why I have called this chapter "A Special Privilege." In 2005, Paul and Karen announced that they were expecting another baby and in December of that year, little Eleanor arrived. She is such a joy to her family and a real blessing to everyone who meets her. A short while after her birth, Paul contacted me and explained that he and Karen would like me to be Eleanor's godmother. I was absolutely thrilled, as you can imagine; Mary's youngest grand-daughter was to be my godchild. That takes some beating! The following June, I travelled with Ian and his family, to Paul's home in Oxfordshire, for Eleanor's Christening. Unfortunately Trevor could not accompany me, as he was committed to a men's conference in Spain. The weekend proved an opportunity to meet close friends of Paul's and Karen's and members of Karen's family, who welcomed me warmly. It was also good to spend precious time with Gill, Thomas, Ian and Jane. But being with the children was particularly special and gave me the chance to get to know my little god-daughter who is needless to say, adorable. The whole weekend was such a happy occasion, the high point being the Christening service on the Sunday morning. Standing next to Paul, I felt a huge sense of fulfilment and joy at being able to make such important vows on behalf of little Eleanor and I shall do my utmost to honour them. Holding her after the service and cuddling her, warmed my heart so much, as did the laughter and fun of her brother and sister and the pleasure they gained from her.

Leaving Oxfordshire later that day, I travelled with Ian and his family back to their home in Yorkshire, where I had left my car. They encouraged me to stay overnight before returning home the next day and we spent a very pleasant evening together. The following morning at breakfast, seven year old Timothy asked me a question which was totally unexpected, but brought me tremendous pleasure.

"Auntie Vivien…will you walk me to school please?" It was such a simple request, but Timothy had no idea how deeply his words would touch me. Thousands of mothers walk their children to school every day and I had done it myself for many years when my boys were little. But this was very different. Hand in hand, Timothy and I strolled down the road towards his school. It was a beautiful day; the sun was already promising to break through the clouds and turning the corner, I could see Timothy's school nestling against the backdrop of the rolling Yorkshire hills. He was chatting all the way and I'm sure he did not notice that I had tears in my eyes, as I remembered his great grandmother (my mother, if you recall) holding Paul's hand whilst walking her young grandson to a different school in a different setting some thirty five years previously. For anyone watching us, it was just an ordinary every day scene; an aunt, walking her great-nephew to school on a perfect summer's day, but for me it was incredibly meaningful, as I marvelled yet again at the way in which things had come full circle. Who but a loving, faithful Father could possibly orchestrate events in this way? God is full of surprises and so much more creative than we realise or credit Him with, arranging circumstances which bless us in ways we would never have imagined. Not only had He been taking care of my heart, but He was setting His seal on what was happening in a tangible way, giving added significance to Isaiah 40:11, the verse quoted at the beginning of this chapter and one which meant so much to me when my sons were young. Like a master artist who with flawless brushstrokes, tenderly restores a priceless painting, so God's desire is to restore His children by touching them unexpectedly with a loving hand and graciously drawing them closer to Himself.

The weekend of Eleanor's Christening will always remain a highlight for me and a short walk with a little boy on that Monday morning, was most definitely 'the icing on the cake.'

25

Moving Our Tent Pegs

"Enlarge the place of your tent, stretch your tent curtains wide, do not hold back; lengthen your cords, strengthen your stakes." (Isaiah 54:2)

"You know, we could do with you two on staff here." This surprise remark was made to Trevor and me during the summer of 2003. We were spending a week at Capernwray Hall, enjoying a programme called "Prime Time," which was geared to the over forties' age group. We were sitting in the courtyard, chatting with Rob Whittaker, the Principal of Capernwray Bible School, when he suddenly made the comment. I thought he was joking, but apparently not. Trevor and I loved visiting Capernwray as guests, but we had never considered working there, nor did we ever anticipate an opportunity to do so. It seemed that Rob saw the need for an older couple to come on board, to fulfil the role of pastoral care workers with the students; in essence, to be a mum and dad to them. It was a role which certainly appealed to me but we needed to be sure that we were hand in hand in making a right decision. Trevor was approaching retirement from his career in Banking and our sons were all independent, so there was no immediate reason why we should not consider a change in direction. Rob suggested that we prayed about it and discussed the possibility with close friends. At this point, I am going to let Trevor write about the amazing way in which God spoke to him.

"Vivien would have accepted the appointment, but I would have been unsure if it would have been the right move for us. I was very settled on the Isle of Man and was working at a job I loved. However, God was preparing my heart in advance of the move. I had bought two large semi detached houses on the island and converted them into six luxury apartments. The work had just been completed and we were going to Capernwray for a much needed rest both physical and spiritual. We were due to travel by boat late on the Friday evening and stay near Liverpool, travelling to Capernwray the next day. That evening a water pipe burst on one of the top floor apartments and water began to flood into the apartments immediately below. Everything was soaked and we had to bail out the water from the ground floor. I decided that we would have to cancel our holiday, but our sons said they would sort out the mess and insisted we go ahead with our plans. By this time it was late in the evening but we drove the car to Douglas, the main port, arriving at 11:30 to catch the 10:30 sailing. The ferry had been delayed and was about to leave. We were able to drive straight onto the boat; the very last car to do so.

We arrived 3 hours later in Liverpool and by the time we reached our hotel, it was about 3:00 a.m. Vivien went to sleep immediately but I lay awake worrying about the damage to the apartments: "Was water lying in the ceiling voids? Would the plasterboard on the walls warp? Would the electrical wiring be affected? Would the carpets shrink as they dried out? Where did the water go when it hit the ground floor apartment?" As I was pondering these questions, I felt God say to me – "Next week, when you hear the name of Adoniram Judson, I am going to speak to you." It happened three times, leaving me in no doubt that God was preparing my heart to hear what He was going to say to me.

Adoniram Judson lived in the 18th century and was a missionary to Burma. He translated the Bible into Burmese and created the first English / Burmese dictionary. I had read his life story thirty years previously and had not heard his name mentioned since, nor had I thought very much about him. I was sure that it was God speaking to me that night. However, I had to wait until the following Friday morning at Capernwray before I understood what was happening.

The speaker that week was the Bible School principal, Rob Whittaker, and he was dealing with the book of Habbakuk. In the middle of his talk, he stopped and suddenly said that he felt the need to mention Adoniram Judson. I was shocked and couldn't wait to hear what God was going to say. Nothing materialised during the remainder of the session and I escaped into the grounds to re-read Habbakuk, assuming that God would be speaking to me through His word. Again disappointment, but on return to the courtyard, Rob asked to speak to both of us and invited us to join the staff. My spirit quickened and I knew that this was what God had prepared for me to hear. We both knew that this was God's call on our lives but it took time before I could accept the leading of the Holy Spirit. A while previously and over a two year period, I had completed pastoral training at evening school, but had not been appointed to the role of pastor in a church, as the timing and circumstances never seemed right. Now, eleven years later, God called me to the role of pastoral worker at a place I loved. It was a wrench to leave the island but we both knew that it was right. As a result, I handed in my resignation at the Bank.

I subsequently asked Rob Whittaker why he had mentioned Adoniram Judson. It was not part of the lecture as such, but God had impressed Rob to make mention of Judson yet he was not aware of the main reason for doing so."

With this confirmation in mind and with the knowledge that our family was backing us one hundred per cent, the decision was made. It was subject to us spending two weeks at Capernwray for a "dummy run," during which time we mixed with students and staff and began to get a feel of what our role would potentially involve. By that stage, the Board had agreed to our appointment and we met with Rob and the registrar Sue Gilmore, to iron out any issues. So in September, 2004, Trevor and I began to work at Capernwray Hall, in the position of pastoral carers. We found a perfect cottage in which to live, about five miles from the Hall. We firmly believe that it was a gift from God, because it became available to us just at the right time. From the back, the cottage overlooks beautiful countryside, where cows roam in the fields and occasionally pop their heads over the stone wall which separates our property from the farmer's land. Squirrels and pheasants frequently visit us in our garden, as do several varieties of birds, depending on the time of year. Brilliant!

Our days at Capernwray are very full and we love the work to which God has called us. In many ways, I feel that everything which came before was a preparation for the ministry we are involved with now. My past circumstances have been a training ground; not just working with the "Stauros Foundation" on the Isle of Man, or "Rebuilders" in Northern Ireland, but more especially, all that I have learnt on my own journey through life. None of it has been wasted. I look back on all that has happened, some of which I would have chosen, some I would definitely not have chosen at the time, but which God allowed in order for His purposes to be fulfilled. He has constantly proved His faithfulness to me, even in the darkest place. Now He has brought me out into the light and to be honest, I feel He has saved the best until last. I have certainly never felt so much that Trevor and I are exactly where God wants us to be and there is such a freedom in knowing that. It means that although the work is often extremely demanding and challenging, we have the resources in Christ to cope. It is also extremely important that we are part of a team and that we are accountable to that team. There is always back-up, should we need it. Over and above their main area of work, all members of the Capernwray Staff are committed to supporting the students and caring for them in any way which is appropriate. However, for Trevor and me, our sole brief is pastoral care. This means that we have so much more time and can be available to the students on an on going basis. In over thirty years of marriage, I have never seen Trevor so fulfilled and that gives me great joy. There is nowhere else that we would rather be and our cottage provides us with a wonderful haven of rest at the end of a busy day.

Having brought up four sons, we are well aware of the pressures which face young people in today's society. The students come from all over the world, but at least half of them are from North America, where it appears to be much more the evangelical culture for young people to spend a year at Bible School. Their ages range from eighteen to fifty plus, with the vast majority being between eighteen and twenty-five. For most, it is their first time away from home and a huge readjustment on every level. Drawn from a broad cross section of cultural backgrounds, many of the students stay for both Winter and Spring School, which gives us the chance to draw very close to them and allow a deep bond to develop. The international flavour of the school is very special and an integral part of its Christian ethos. Staff and students learn a great deal from being with so many different nationalities and for many, it is a life changing experience.

I look back at my journey over the years and see the way that God has been setting things in place for me, gently steering me in the direction of my present role; one which I find so rewarding and enriching. I am also conscious that He has been drawing me closer to His heart, teaching me what it really means to live in the reality of His presence each day and to be increasingly aware of the freedom which that brings. In fact, I think it all comes down to the powerful and over-riding truth of what freedom in Christ really means. I believe we misunderstand freedom. We chase after an impostor who masquerades in many forms, leaving us feeling cheated, disillusioned and trapped. But true freedom implies being rescued. It is the most precious of all gifts offered by the Rescuer; it has a dimension and a depth of reality nothing else can touch. When we discover it, we discover the potential to be true to ourselves in all our relationships. This freedom gives us our identity and energises the soul with a dynamic and a vitality beyond our expectation. It is an integral part of our inheritance in Christ, linked implicitly with redemption, wholeness and well-being. I wish I could have understood that without having to travel a painful, rocky road from time to time, but that's how we learn isn't it?

In his book "The Problem of Pain." C.S.Lewis writes,

"God whispers in our pleasures, speaks to us in our conscience, but shouts in our pain. It is His megaphone to rouse a deaf world." Certainly, there have been many times when I have been deaf.

I am not sure how long I shall continue fulfilling my role at Capernwray. But I hope that it will be for a few more years at least. However, I am conscious that I don't really need to know; nor should I anticipate or worry about what the future might hold. It is enough that my Father knows. I can embrace the present; trusting that my journey here on earth is not yet over…..but then, neither my fellow traveller is yours.

"The Lord your God, who is going before you, will fight for you, as he did for you in Egypt, before your very eyes and in the desert. There you saw how the Lord your God carried you, as a father carries his son, all the way you went until you reached this place." (Deut. 1:30-31).

Evangelical Ministries
103-113 Ravenhill Road
Belfast
BT6 8DR

Telephone: 028 9045 5400
Web site: *www.emins.com*

Stauros Foundation
Ballyards Castle
123 Keady Road
Armagh
BT60 3AD

Telephone: 028 3752 7124
Web site: *www.stauros.com*

Capernwray Hall
Carnforth
Lancashire
LA6 1AG

Telephone: 01524 733908
Web site: *www.capernwray.org.uk*